The Dark Double

THE DARK DOUBLE

US Media, Russia, and the Politics of Values

ANDREI P. TSYGANKOV

Oxford University Press is a department of the University of Oxford. It furthers
the University's objective of excellence in research, scholarship, and education
by publishing worldwide. Oxford is a registered trade mark of Oxford University
Press in the UK and certain other countries.

Published in the United States of America by Oxford University Press
198 Madison Avenue, New York, NY 10016, United States of America.

© Oxford University Press 2019

All rights reserved. No part of this publication may be reproduced, stored in
a retrieval system, or transmitted, in any form or by any means, without the
prior permission in writing of Oxford University Press, or as expressly permitted
by law, by license, or under terms agreed with the appropriate reproduction
rights organization. Inquiries concerning reproduction outside the scope of the
above should be sent to the Rights Department, Oxford University Press, at the
address above.

You must not circulate this work in any other form
and you must impose this same condition on any acquirer.

CIP data is on file at the Library of Congress
ISBN 978–0–19–091934–4 (pbk.)
ISBN 978–0–19–091933–7 (hbk.)

We often perceive others, be they individuals, groups, or even the whole societies, as simply "good" or "bad." Once this fateful decision is made, the rest is easy, for the "good" person or group can have only desirable social characteristics and the "bad" can have only reprehensible traits. And once such evaluative stability of social perception is established, it is extremely difficult to alter. . . .

[T]his tendency to regress to simple categories of perception is especially strong under conditions of emotional stress and external threat.

—Uri Bronfenbrenner, "The Mirror Image in Soviet-American Relations," 50.

CONTENTS

List of Illustrations — ix
Preface — xi

1. Values and Media in US-Russia Relations — 1
   US-Russia Relations in the Realm of Values — 2
   Explaining US Media Biases — 9
   The Book's Organization — 13

2. Fears of Russia, Suppressed and Revealed — 17
   National Fears, Media, and State — 17
   American Fears of Russia — 23
   The Role of Government — 28

3. American "Universal" Values and Russia — 33
   Russia in "Transition": The Early 1990s — 33
   Russia in "Chaos": 1995–2005 — 36
   "Neo-Soviet Autocracy": 2005–2013 — 38
   Value Differences and Interstate Tensions — 44
   "Foreign Enemy": 2014–2016 — 52
   Conclusion — 56

4. Russia Fights Back — 57
   Is Russia Blameless? — 58
   From Acceptance to Containment of American Values — 64
   Why Russia Is "Anti-American" — 72

5. Russophobia in the Age of Donald Trump — 81
   - The Narrative of Trump's "Collusion" with Russia — 82
   - Opposition to the "Collusion" Narrative — 86
   - Explaining Russophobia — 89
   - Russia's Role and Motives — 93

6. Conclusion — 97
   - American Values and Russia — 97
   - Is Russia Doomed to Be the Dark Double? — 100
   - Future Clashes of Values — 105

Notes — 111
Bibliography — 139
Index — 153

ILLUSTRATIONS

Figures

2.1. Values, Interstate Relations, and Media — 23
3.1. The US Media Perception of Russia, 2000–2014 — 40
4.1. The US and Russian Media Perceptions of Each Other, 2008–2015 — 68

Tables

2.1. US Values, Interstate Relations, and Media Views of Russia — 32
3.1. The US Media Frames of Russia — 45
4.1. The Russian Media Frames of the United States, 2007–2015 — 72

PREFACE

This book grew out of several related projects on values, emotions, and the media's role in shaping Russia's and America's international actions and perceptions.

In fall 2013, while on sabbatical from teaching, I researched the topic of Russia's distinct "civilizational" values. My interests were well served by a two-month fellowship at the University of Helsinki's Aleksanteri Institute, where I had the pleasure of stimulating interactions with colleagues, participated in the Europe-wide conference "Russia and the World," and presented preliminary results of my research at the Aleksanteri seminar. At Vyacheslav Morozov's invitation, I further presented my findings at the University of Tartu, Estonia. During October of the same year, I traveled to Moscow and was fortunate to interview some of those in Russia who intellectually prepared the country's turn to distinct values, including by contributing to Vladimir Putin's speeches since his election campaign in early 2012.

While developing my interest in values, I took part in a project on emotions in Russian foreign policy, which further influenced my thinking. The project was organized by Reinhard Wolf at Goethe University, Frankfurt am Main, Germany, Regina Heller at the University of Hamburg, Germany, and Tuomas Forsberg at the University of Tampere, Finland. I thank them all for inviting me into the project and giving me the opportunity to interact with an excellent international group of scholars and expand my understanding of the role of emotions and moral beliefs in foreign policy.

During the 2014–2015 academic year I benefited from a grant at San Francisco State University to study US-Russia relations in the realm of values, which allowed me to concentrate on understanding the role of media in these relations. I gratefully acknowledge the financial support of the Office of Academic Programs and research assistance by Greg Sherman. Matthew Tarver-Wahlquist offered editorial assistance and helped with proofreading my work.

My understanding of media narratives was also assisted by participation in the project on digital Eurasia organized by Mark Bassin and Mikhail Suslov at Suderstrom University and Uppsala University, respectively.

In October 2015 I participated in the annual forum of the Valdai Discussion Club. I thank Andrei Bystritsky, Timofei Bordachev, Fyodor Lukyanov, Andrei Sushentsov, and all those involved in organizing this excellent conference for international affairs experts and for making my participation possible. I thank the mentioned individuals, as well as Sergei Karaganov, Andrei Kortunov, Olga Malinova, Boris Mezhuyev, Nikolai Rabotyazhev, Eduard Solovyev, Dmitry Suslov, Ivan Timofeev, Pavel Tsygankov, and Igor Zevelev for discussing with me some of the ideas expressed in this book.

While at the Valdai forum I was fortunate to ask Vladimir Putin a question about the role of values in US-Russia relations. Putin's answer was illuminating in revealing his thinking on Russian "civilizational" values. In particular, I asked whether the growing polarization between the Russian image of the West as spiritually corrupt and the Western image of Russia as the oppressive neo-Soviet autocracy reflect the inevitable struggle between culturally distinct entities. Putin's reply confirmed the perception by the Kremlin of the superiority of Russian values, yet it also made clear that in the view of the president the clash of values results less from cultural difference than from frequently lacking respect and recognition of each other's autonomy:

> If we look at ideas among our thinkers, philosophers, writers, they associate conflicts between Russia and the West with broad differences in worldviews. And they are partially correct. Russia's worldview is based upon notions of good and evil, higher forces, and God's will. However, the Western worldview—and I don't mean it in derogatory way—is based upon individual interest, pragmatism, and pragmatic accommodation.
>
> . . . It is hard for us to conduct a dialogue with those who are guided by ideas of messianism and exceptionalism because this means a radical departure from our common traditional values as founded on God-given equality. This does not mean that we cannot look for ways to interact. We will continue to do so.
>
> . . . If some parts of American society feel friendship or love toward Russia, then they should explain to the rest of the society in the United States and to those who make political decisions that Russia ought to be treated with respect.[1]

I argue in the book that these two dimensions—cultural difference and lack of political respect for the other—shape and inform media perception and interstate competition in the realm of values. One should view those as mutually related and not isolated from each other. Cultural and historically developed perceptions shape and inform international relations but become sources of international conflicts in the context of (geo)political competition.

Parts of several chapters draw on my previously published article "The Neo-Soviet Autocracy," *Politics*, 2016, and books *Russia's Foreign Policy* (Lanham, MD: Rowman & Littlefield, 2006), *Russophobia: Anti-Russian Lobby and American Foreign*

Policy (London: Palgrave, 2009), and *The Strong State in Russia* (New York: Oxford University Press, 2014). I thank the publishers for permission to use these materials in the book.

At Oxford University Press, I am especially grateful to David McBride for his faith in the project, guidance, and patience. I am also thankful to all those at the press performing editorial services and preparing the manuscript for publication.

In addition to the above-mentioned people, I greatly benefited from comments and reactions by anonymous reviewers. These comments and reactions were essential in improving the book. One reviewer provided especially penetrating commentaries and suggested that I write a follow-up on my *Russophobia* as a sustained critique of the US media's perception of Russia.

The resulting book is less about special interest groups with anti-Russian agendas in the Washington establishment than about media narratives, frames, and confrontational presentations of Russia. The book is also about the media's interaction with the US government and the official perception of Russia, which in the mid-2000s was more moderate than that of the media, but has since 2012 converged with the media's hostile presentation of Russia. Gradually the US government that sought to increase political pressures on the Kremlin to change its foreign policy embraced the media's confrontational perception of Russia as threatening American values.

While researching and writing the book, I took part in multiple conferences in the United States, Europe, Russia, and China and interacted with students and colleagues at my home university and outside. I appreciate all of their valuable insights and, needless to say, am alone responsible for the book's content and conclusions.

My final word of gratitude is always to my family. My parents and my wife Julia have been a constant source of encouragement and inspiration. The increasingly conflictual relations between the

United States and Russia have had a deep impact on our hearts and minds. For many years Julia has been the first to patiently listen to my thoughts and impressions about Western political and media culture and to offer a common-sense reaction and support. I dedicate this book to her and to all those with the ability to cut through the fog of the media's prejudices and to remain skeptical in these highly politicized times.

In transliterating names from the Russian, I have used "y" to denote "ы," ' to denote "ь" and "ъ," "yu" to denote "ю," "ya" to denote "я," "i" to denote "й" and "ий," "iyi" to denote double "и," "e" to denote "э," "kh" to denote "х," "zh" to denote "ж," "ts" to denote "ц," "ch" to denote "ч," "sh" to denote "ш," and "sch" to denote "щ." I have also used "Ye" to distinguish the sound of "e" (such as "Yevropa") in the beginning of a word from that in the middle of a word (such as "vneshnei"). I do not distinguish between "e" and "ë." Spelling is retained in quotations.

The Dark Double

1
Values and Media in US-Russia Relations

In the course of history and international relations, each political community develops a particular system of values. Values are culturally and historically established beliefs about the appropriate organization of human institutions and foreign policy.[1] Such beliefs are cognitive because repetitive social practices reinforce them as "truths." Yet these beliefs are also deeply emotional because they set standards of right and wrong, serve as moral purposes,[2] and constitute the commitment to uphold certain rules and principles. As Karl Manheim argued some century ago, *"Politics as politics is possible only as long* as the realm of the irrational still exists."[3] Overall, values act as lenses though which human communities form international perceptions and assess interests.

The US-Russia relationship is an appropriate ground for understanding the role that values and media play in both cooperation and conflict between two nations. Although these relations have been commonly analyzed as reflecting elites' political and economic preferences,[4] such preferences frequently reflect nationwide beliefs as accentuated and radicalized by different media systems. Scholars of ideas and national identity have studied how both countries' foreign policies have expressed their historically developed images, beliefs, and emotions,[5] and how their interaction has resulted in misperceptions and biases in viewing each other.[6]

US-Russia Relations in the Realm of Values

Historically, Western nations have built competitive political systems with checks and balances and popular elections of public officials, whereas many non-Western societies, including Russia, have relied on a highly centralized and concentrated authority of the executive.[7] During the Cold War, US authorities, media, and popular culture often presented this value difference in highly ideological terms—as an irreconcilable struggle between good and evil. Americans predominantly defined themselves through the Soviet "other,"[8] viewing their country's values as incomparably superior to and more legitimate than those of the USSR. America was the land of freedom and law, whereas the Soviet state was the oppressive empire that sought to dominate neighbors through force. As the historian David Foglesong wrote, ever since the late nineteenth century, influential circles in the United States have viewed Russia as their "dark double"—disrespectful of religious freedoms and property rights and an object of ideological transformation.[9] The Bolshevik revolution in 1917 and the Cold War served to strengthen such perceptions of Russia in the West, reinforcing some of the old fears of the country.

Over the last thirty years, US-Russia relations in the realm of values went full circle from confrontation between "communism" and "capitalism" under the Cold War to convergence, growing divergence, and then a return to confrontation that a number of observers view as a new cold war.[10]

Following the Cold War, the United States ceased to view Russia and its values as threatening. Rather, the perception developed that the new Russia was becoming a part of the West, embracing its ideas and governing principles. The end of the Cold War was interpreted as a victory of the West's "universal" values. Russia's leaders at the time themselves proclaimed their commitment to such values and sought to integrate with Western economic and security institutions. In their own words, Russia was becoming "normal" again and was eager to reunite with the West. For instance, Russia's first foreign minister, Andrei Kozyrev, stated that the country's system of values was to change, as Russia was to accept the priority of the individual and the free market over society and state and develop a "natural partnership" with Western countries.[11]

However, the contestation of values did not end with the Cold War. Although the old ideological dichotomy of "communism" and "capitalism" was past, the two nations were increasingly at odds in how they viewed each other. By the mid-1990s, it became clear that Russia was not converging with Western values. Although the country abandoned the old Soviet system, Russia also began to reproduce familiar strong-state principles with a highly concentrated authority of the executive and few checks and balances. The new 1993 constitution consolidated these principles by giving the president a level of power comparable with that of the Russian tsars. During the 2000s, Vladimir Putin continued to consolidate state power as the country's new president, acting on the belief that "a strong state is not anomaly that should be gotten rid of . . . [but] a source and guarantor of order and the initiator and main driving force of any change."[12]

In the United States, the perception of Russia as threatening American values appeared in the mid-2000s and was articulated by various groups in Washington and the mainstream media.[13] Responding to multiple developments in Russia's domestic and foreign policy, the US media introduced the narrative of a neo-Soviet autocracy, according to which everything in the country is controlled by Vladimir Putin, who acts from the perception of America as the main enemy. The narrative of a neo-Soviet Russia had existed in the United States since the Cold War end, but until the mid-2000s it did not dominate the media space. Now some seasoned observers were describing the new perception of Russia in the media "as a concerted effort to alienate Russia from the West"[14] and displaying an attitude that was "more anti-Russian than was our policy toward Soviet communist Russia."[15]

Leading US newspapers and TV networks presented a view of Russia in which an authoritarian police state was systematically eliminating political opposition, harassing foreigners and minorities, and aggressively vilifying the United States. Those developments inside Russia that did not fit this binary narrative received little media coverage. For instance, the mainstream media rarely reported on the revival of Christian faith in the country, struggles with corruption, or attempts to strengthen relations with neighbors and Western nations. By contrast, the American economic and political system was presented as incomparably superior and largely devoid of serious problems. With respect to practical relations with Russia, the media's advice for US policymakers was consistently on the side of exerting pressures on the Kremlin and containing its international "expansion," rather than proposing cooperation and joint solutions.[16]

These aspects of the media's perception of Russia were reflected in US policy changes. Following the Cold War's end, the United States shifted from a policy of containment toward one of integrating Russia on the West's terms. Russia was expected to become a market economy and Western-style liberal democracy. During the 2000s, Russia was not yet perceived as a "threat," but was no longer "a nation in hopeful transition."[17] A number of prominent US officials were increasingly worried about Russia getting "off track" and the country's potential to oppose America's world leadership. After all, Russia was the only nuclear power capable of challenging the United States. Already in 2000 a prominent review of US defense policy argued that reducing the nuclear force was likely to be dangerous. Instead, the report favored the expansion of military capabilities.[18]

Despite a period when other priorities appeared to take center stage in the relationship, the move away from attempts to integrate Russia continued, with values increasingly becoming a central issue in bilateral relations. The White House did not prioritize the issue of values even when George W. Bush launched the global strategy of regime change following the Iraq War in 2003. Rather, the focus was on addressing vital issues of international security, including terrorism, nuclear arms control, and regional stability. During his first term, Barack Obama rarely commented on Russia's domestic politics and concentrated on building relations with then-president Dmitry Medvedev in order to jointly tackle issues of nuclear arms control. However, after 2011 and especially following his election for the second term, Obama revised his perception of Russia by increasingly stressing the importance of values and pressing the Kremlin on human rights issues. The media narrative of Russia as a threat to Western values converged with the language of US officials, many of whom now viewed Russia as a hostile, undemocratic regime.

The new policy in Washington was to directly challenge Putin on his actions at home and strengthen ties with his domestic critics and liberal Russian media. When the new American ambassador to Russia, Michael McFaul, arrived to Moscow in January 2012, he explained that he intend to "sell our policy" in "a very, very aggressive way."[19] Although the approach had already been met with a negative reaction in Russia, on the second day of his work McFaul attended a meeting with opposition figures. The meeting was prearranged by his predecessors but was widely perceived in

Russia as the first in a series of actions aiming to overthrow Putin and replace him with a US-favored politician.

Following the Euromaidan revolution and the change of power in Ukraine in February 2014, the official US rhetoric toward Russia became indistinguishable from that of the American media. The White House was no longer restrained in its comments on Putin, and on several occasions referred to him as a corrupt, autocratic leader[20] who clings to power by intimidating "neighbors not out of strength but out of weakness."[21] McFaul, who by that time had left Russia as the US ambassador, called on the West to confront and isolate "Putin's Russia" by replicating the Cold War struggle with the Soviet Union.[22] In response to Russia's annexation of Crimea and support for eastern Ukrainian separatists, the United States imposed heavy sanctions against the Russian economy, seeking to contain the Kremlin's expansionism.

Under President Donald Trump, US-Russia relations entered a new period. Trump's election revealed a major divide over values within American society. Whereas his opponents remained committed to a world order based on liberal institutionalist ideas, Trump favored a return to military strength, unilateralism, and economic nationalism.[23] During the election campaign, he took issues with liberal characterizations of Russia as an "enemy" to be contained and argued for lifting sanctions and building partnership with Moscow on the basis of counterterrorism. In response, liberal media attacked Trump as an autocracy-leaning Putin proxy.[24]

The Russia issue became central in the new internal divide between the Trump administration and the liberal establishment. The United States' intelligence agencies concluded that the Kremlin interfered in America's presidential elections.[25] The new consensus within the mainstream liberal media and political class was that Trump reflected non-American values[26] and that he was likely in "collusion" with Russia. Long before Special

Counsel Robert Mueller launched, let alone completed, investigation of Trump's connection to the Kremlin, some *New York Times* columnists had already assumed that Trump was the "Siberian" candidate.[27]

Not all media commentators shared the dominant perspective on Russia. Voices of dissent included those on political left and right who questioned the idea of vilifying Russia and demonizing its president. Media critics included Professor Stephen F. Cohen, winners of the Pulitzer Prize and other journalistic awards Glenn Greenwald and Robert Parry, prominent politician and former presidential candidate Patrick Buchanan, the US ambassador to the USSR, Jack Matlock, and others.[28] These critics, however, rarely appeared in mainstream media publishing in outlets such as *American Conservative*, Antiwar.com, the Consortiumnews.com, *CounterPunch*, *Intercept*, *The Nation*, and the like. Their work, while important, was not able to shake the formed consensus in media and political circles. Instead of being receptive to alternative viewpoints, mainstream commentators ignored or attacked dissidents as unpatriotic apologists for Putin.[29] Exceptions were not made even for those within the mainstream whose views began to deviate from the consensus.[30]

These developments indicate that focusing on values and media is essential for understanding US-Russia relations. Values serve as a powerful, independent, even decisive source of human action. They are not permanently established entities and are best understood in conjunction with the politics of media and state.[31] If the two countries are to move beyond viewing each other as potential enemies, they must find a way to reframe their values in nonconfrontational terms. Nevertheless, in contrast to the practice in some common explanations of US-Russia relations, values should not be reduced to the considerations of state interests, power, and domestic politics.

Of the politics-centered explanations, some stress international competition for power, while others focus on domestic political struggles. The international competition approach views values and media as following state geopolitical preferences. Its supporters argue that projects of cultural attractiveness or "soft power" are increasingly framed in politically competitive terms[32] and that Russia's rejection of liberal values reflects the Kremlin's desire to protect itself from Western promotion of democracy.[33] The domestic politics approach draws attention to the internal vulnerabilities of Putin's regime and its dependence on diversionary politics and the image of an external enemy,[34] as well as to various groups with anti-Russian agendas constraining the United States' government in its relations with Moscow.[35]

The described approaches are right to identify the politically competitive side of value-based relations, yet they tend to underestimate cultural and historically developed sources of international conflicts. For instance, according to public polls, Americans and Russians became disappointed in each other's values *before* the White House and the Kremlin chose to prioritize the issue in their relations during the 2010s. In the United States, the percentage of those viewing Russia unfavorably has gone up since the mid-2000s, exceeding 50% in 2009,[36] whereas anti-American attitudes in Russia increased since 2003, reaching 50% in 2005.[37] While state participation was necessary for the cultural conflict to occur, it was not sufficient.

Being formed by long-term historical experiences, values are not easily manipulated by politicians with narrow and partisan agendas. Politicians do not operate in a social vacuum. In mass-market societies, they cannot ignore public emotions and value preferences as articulated by media. Politicians are genuinely effective in achieving their objectives only when they have a high level of public support. For example, while the Kremlin indeed launched a media campaign to discredit its domestic and external opponents, particularly following the Ukraine crisis, such a campaign would have not been successful without the audience's support.[38]

Explaining US Media Biases

Scholars have long established that media serve important social functions. Along with other cultural institutions such as art, cinema, literature, and science, the media validate, develop, or challenge various collectively held values, prejudices, and stereotypes. From a socially constructivist perspective, mass media are an essential contributor to a presentation of popular identity that then shapes formation of critically important international decisions.[39] The media do so by covering and interpreting daily news. Even when media strive to be independent by offering "objective" reporting and promoting a neutral viewpoint in public discussions, they do so under particular cultural constraints and within particular boundaries of historically formed social values. Indeed, as Kari Hafez has argued, globalization has not fundamentally changed the dominance of local and nationally oriented mainstream media that remain deeply connected to local identity structures and narratives.[40]

The media's centeredness on dominant national values, or ethnocentrism, is well established. An ethnocentric perception of the world is defined as the belief that one's own culture represents the natural and best way to do things.[41] Such a perception is often established through social narratives that connect everyday events and situations into a larger picture with a coherent structure, a clear sense of actors, and moral virtues to uphold. Narratives are based on visions of the self, the other, and their relationships.[42] In his classic works *Orientalism* and *Covering Islam*, Edward Said has documented a series of ethnocentric assumptions underlying

Western perception and media analysis of "the Orient." According to Said, European and American media have not infrequently associated Islam with religious radicalism, terrorism, and oppressive regimes.[43] Such representations support the dominant narrative of the West as the land of tolerance and liberalism.

In competitive political systems such as the United States, where a fully centralized control of information is impossible, media possess a degree of autonomy. The national community is rarely uniform, and media participate in discussions of values by adopting a particular way of framing news. Frames are presentations of the self and the other through various images, metaphors, and ethical categories that help to communicate the larger narrative to its social audience.[44] Distinct images of the "other" may serve as framing devises that connect facts to political discourse and policymakers' worldviews.[45]

However, when national values are challenged from outside, the national space for contestation and self-criticism shrinks, giving way to attitudes of superiority and defensiveness. National confidence declines, and fears and negative stereotypes rise. In a world of global information, there are many examples of the media's perpetuating prejudices and operating on the fears of others. Popular discomfort with uncertainty and anxiety may translate into intolerance. Such examples range from the Islamophobia in Danish and French cartoons that depicted the Prophet, Mohammed, as a terrorist, to the most virulent forms of anti-Americanism in non-Western societies. Under increased international competition, states are also pressured to present themselves as defenders of national values and traditions and are tempted to engage in nationalist mythmaking, fearmongering, and strategic cover-ups.[46]

It is therefore simplistic to view media as fully dependent on manipulations by government officials, as is argued in some studies. For instance, the so-called propaganda model presents the

US media as spreading and perpetuating the dominant ideological assumptions.[47] Although governments are contributors to media presentations of events, governments are constrained in their actions by international developments and the media's institutional autonomy. Media may or may not "follow the flag" depending on how informed they are and how the social audience perceives news. However, media tend to follow the state presentation of events directly when perceived national values are externally challenged and when media are dependent on the government for information.

The US media biases on Russia have roots in clashes of cultural values as influenced by interstate and domestic politics. Allies for some periods and enemies for others, the two sides have not overcome some of the old perceptions, stereotypes, and emotions, viewing each other as potentially dangerous. The Russian system of values has been established as culturally distinct. It includes a deeply held concept of spiritual freedom inspired by Eastern Christianity and the idea of a strong, socially protective state capable of defending its own subjects from abuses at home and threats from abroad. Russia expects the United States to recognize these values as legitimate and cooperates with Western nations when its fundamental values and interests are not challenged. In the absence of such external recognition, the Russian state gains sufficient national support to turn to a nationalist and assertive foreign policy, especially when it possesses sufficient power capabilities.[48]

The US values are quite distinct from those of Russia. Divergent religious influences, geography, and international relations are responsible for the divergence. Distinct spiritual traditions—Protestantism and Eastern Christianity—formed individualistic and communal mentalities, respectively. Founded by European pilgrims of Protestant origins, the United States has historically proceeded from ideas of individual salvation. The Enlightenment-influenced conception of religious freedom[49] and spiritually grounded individualism informed American state-building practices and the establishment of a constitutional state with specially designed checks and balances within the political system. Later, in the course of World War II, these ideas took on the new meaning of being universally applicable in organizing human societies.

The two countries' value systems came into conflict due to growing interstate competition. The United States emerged as the dominant power following World War II and sought to expand its global presence, whereas the Soviet Union wanted to strengthen its international position, particularly in Europe. Driven by global and regional geopolitical ambitions, the United States and the Soviet Union each presented their political systems as ideologically incompatible. The two countries' media were active participants in presenting each other's values as unacceptable. The situation was less conflictual under periods of relative international stability, particularly before the October Revolution in 1917, following the US recognition of the USSR in 1933, and during the cooperation in war against Nazi Germany.

A similar value clash developed following the end of the Cold War. The United States' sense of overwhelming power in the international system led to a hegemonic foreign policy and insistence on the universal applicability of its "democratic values." Russia's resistance to these policies and ideological discourse generated suspicions on the part of American media. Russia's own internal and media politics contributed to the development of these suspicions. In Russia, the state is able to influence media in a more profound way than in the United States.[50] While the US media shaped the discourse on the Russian threat, prompting the state to adjust to it, in Russia the process was the opposite. In response to perceived Western pressures, the Russian state led the way by orchestrating anti-American propaganda in state-controlled media.

The process was more top-down than bottom-up. These political developments in Russia eventually enlisted the US state in support of American "universal" values against Putin's "neo-Soviet" system. Accentuated and politicized by national media, values became a hostage in a struggle for international power.

The Book's Organization

The book seeks to understand the role of US media in presenting American values as principally different from and superior to those of Russia. In order to assess media perceptions, I survey various types of media, analyzing their main themes, as well as the substance and degree of criticism of the Russian side by the US media. In determining media frames in presenting the other, I rely on textual analysis of selected mainstream newspapers in the United States, supplemented by a survey of other media sources.

The book is organized into four parts. Chapter 2 continues with the discussion of national fears and the role of media in the context of the United States' views of Russia. I develop a framework for understanding the US perception and describe fears of Russia in the media as rooted in substantive differences between national visions of the American dream and the Russian Idea and in polarizing political discourses stemming from tensions in the two countries' relations.

Chapter 3 describes in greater detail the Russia discourse in American mainstream media. I argue that the space for debating Russia in the media has narrowed considerably since the mid-2000s, when Russia's political system began to be viewed as a nondemocratic and increasingly anti-Western regime—a point that has been acknowledged by a number of American observers. Critical voices rarely publish in mainstream liberal media to challenge the consensus perspective on Russia. According to such a perspective,

Russia's values are incompatible with and inferior to those of the United States, which renders relations with the Kremlin difficult, if not impossible. In the 2010s, US officials adopted this view partly from media influence and partly out of their own frustration with the Kremlin's policies.

Chapter 4 addresses the Russian side of the story. I argue that Russia is partly responsible for its hostile perception by the US media. The Kremlin's actions, including laws preventing gays and lesbians from speaking publicly, criminal trials of some of government's critics, corruption, election falsifications, and assertive foreign policy have contributed to such perceptions. The issue is the proportion and nuances of such criticism. Although the American media present the Kremlin's "autocracy" as a corrupt and oppressive system, Russia's political system, with all its flaws, is capable of addressing the country's problems. I also question the prudence of the United States' presentation of other nations' values as fundamentally threatening to those of America, particularly when they do not result in egregious examples of violence. Finally, the chapter discusses Russia's own reactions to its presentation in the United States. I argue that Russia's growing anti-Americanism is reactive and dependent on pressure from the United States.

Chapter 5 extends the argument about media and value conflict between Russia and the United States to the age of Donald Trump. I assess the new conflict as especially acute and exacerbated by the US partisan divide. In addition to explaining the new wave of American Russophobia, I analyze Russia's own role and motives. I maintain that media are likely to continue the ideological and largely negative coverage of Russia, especially if Washington and Moscow fail to develop a pragmatic form of cooperation.

The conclusion summarizes the argument and assesses the potential for future cultural conflicts in world politics. I argue that cultural and political divides come from different sources, but in times of internal uncertainty and acute interstate competition, culture and politics tend to reinforce each other, exacerbating international tensions. US-Russia relations may gradually become less dependent on presenting each other as potential ideological threats if the two nations learn to reframe bilateral relations in value-free terms.

2

Fears of Russia, Suppressed and Revealed

National Fears, Media, and State

Every nation is founded on and upheld by certain ideas or values that help to manage diversity and preserve national unity. Such ideas establish a nation's fundamental beliefs, emotions, and orientations regarding the outside world. Values also prescribe relationships between the core and minority groups within a nation, as well as between the unified national self and the outside world. From the perspective of a national community's members, values establish the universe of meanings that bind this community together. Although scholars frequently view human actions as if they were designed to meet rationally determined objectives, it is beliefs and emotions that define the appropriate behavior toward the relevant other.[1] Humans tend to display attitudes of ethnocentrism and are not easily turned to accepting values that have not been central to their own socialization.[2]

With ethnocentric values come emotions and attitudes of not only love and affection for others, but also suspicion and fear. Self-centrism and other-phobia are therefore two sides of the same coin, constituting the inner and outer expressions of a group's values. These attitudes of suspicion and fear are difficult to change. As humans overcome external challenges, they develop common bonds with some and enter into conflicts with others. The developed perceptions of affection and fear may have deep historic roots due to memories of hostilities, conflicts, and humiliations. Experiences of mistreatment constitute national traumas that complicate the establishment of cooperation in international relations.[3]

These negative memories tend to be reinforced by the modern conditions of exclusive territorial states and the competitive nature of international relations.[4] Old traumas and phobias may be activated and sustained by interstate competition. An increased level of such competition may result in global instability, thus generating various anxieties and dislocations in people's consciousness. These processes affect people's emotional, cognitive, and evaluative orientations by encouraging them to identify with habitual national beliefs and the self's perceptions of right and wrong.[5]

Whether the described fears of others are suppressed or revealed depends on the nature of interstate relations and the position assumed by influential media. Perceived historical traumas and cultural phobias are likely to be suppressed and partially healed when governments signal their openness to cooperation with others and when others are prepared to engage in reciprocal relations. Alternatively, hostilities and attitudes of criticism expressed by states toward others are likely to assist in activating previously suppressed fears and prejudices.

The media's role is of additional critical importance. As organs for articulating and promoting values, the media are among the first to identify challenges and threats to such values' existence. Under conditions of political uncertainty and contestation, the media make choices by prioritizing some issues over others and selecting frames that they find appropriate for covering issues. As Manuel Castells writes, "What does not exist in the media does not exist in the public mind, even if it could have a fragmented presence in individual minds . . . the media are not the holders of power, but they constitute by and large the space where power is decided."[6]

As a relatively open space, national media may express diverse views, including with respect to government policies. For instance, in the Russia of the early 2000s, there was a wide-ranging debate between those who advocated for a greater openness to the West and those stressing national distinctiveness. Following the Kremlin's decision to support the United States in the post–September 11 struggle against terrorism, Russian liberal media endorsed the decision as a "choice in favor of a long-term unity with Western or European civilization, of which Russia is an organic part."[7] Other, equally influential media presented the choice as dangerous, leading to Russian "encirclement" by the US and NATO troops. Even the newspaper of the Russian government, *Rossiyskaya gazeta*, rang the alarm: "One way or another Russia, like the entire former USSR, remains encircled by a dense ring of military and intelligence-gathering installations belonging to the North Atlantic alliance."[8] Of special importance was a series of published "open letters" signed by retired generals, including one of Yeltsin's former defense ministers, accusing Putin of "selling out" the country and "betraying" the nation's vital interests.[9]

In other cases when the perceived outside threat is significant and government is not open to international cooperation, the media are likely to be more uniform in expressing negative attitudes toward outsiders. A case in point is Russian media views during interstate crises with the West. For example, during the Yugoslavia crisis, relatively liberal newspapers such as *Izvestia* and *Nezavisimaya gazeta* were critical of NATO's intervention and warned against further alienating Russia from the West. While displaying a diversity of views, various media converged on the idea that NATO's military campaign was illegitimate, set a dangerous precedent, and was potentially destabilizing for the international system as a whole. As an alternative course of action, Russian media favored relying on the United Nations, developing a greater dialogue among existing cultures, and increasing Russia's role in maintaining peace and stability in world affairs.[10] Russian media also displayed generally negative perceptions of the United States during the worsening bilateral relations since roughly 2008. Most media sources dismissed Western criticisms of Russia as emotionally driven and politically calculative propaganda that reflected the general public perception.[11]

As a contested and a relatively pluralist space, media are frequently exploited by special interests and groups with particular agendas, fears, and prejudices. Acting in a favorable environment, political entrepreneurs may be able to rally nationalist feelings and add pressures on the government to engage in confrontational policy with the outside world. However, such lobbying is most effective when outside powers themselves are not seeking international cooperation. Other conditions that strengthen the influence of ethno-phobic lobbies include decline of national confidence, weak political leadership, an uninformed public, and the preferences of an individual outlet's editors.[12]

Media pluralism notwithstanding, it is subject to influence and manipulation by the government. Scholars have documented the ties of media to political elites and the mechanisms of obtaining media support for a particular state narrative. For instance, W. Lance Bennett has demonstrated that mainstream journalists follow elites' agendas, sources, and ways of framing international affairs by *indexing* news coverage to fit debates within Washington so as not to upset major political and economic interests.[13] Others mechanisms of obtaining mass-media support may include journalistic dependence on state-possessed information, commitment to particular ideological beliefs, and the state's own efforts to lobby for particular news coverage. For instance, following the Soviet breakup, the American media discourse assumed that a worldwide progression of US values was in underway. After President George Bush legitimized in his State of the Union address the view that the United States had "won" the Cold War, the dominant US media began to cover the world from this victor's standpoint—a perspective that was reinforced by activities of various groups with special global interests.

In some cases government and media tend to reinforce each other's influences. A case in point is the role played by Rupert Murdoch, the editor of 175 media holdings, all of which supported President George W. Bush and Prime Minister Tony Blair's promotion of the Iraq War. The campaign reflected Murdoch's support for the state and reflected his own views, closely associated with US neoconservatives.[14] As the British newspaper *Guardian* opined, "After an exhaustive survey of the highest-selling and most influential papers across the world owned by Murdoch's News Corporation, it is clear that all are singing from the same hymn sheet. Some are bellicose baritone soloists who relish the fight. Some prefer a less strident, if more subtle, role in the chorus. But none, whether fortissimo or pianissimo, has dared to croon the anti-war tune. Their master's voice has never been questioned."[15]

In addition to tactical ways of influencing media, most governments develop *strategies* for working with media and managing global information. Political power tends to engage in strategical games of exclusion and inclusion with respect to various cultural communities at home and abroad. Some of these strategies work to suppress national suspicions and fears, while others capitalize on those. One such strategy is that of influence, or soft power.¹⁶ The strategy of influence proceeds from national confidence and is not based on the politics of fear. Rather, it seeks to transmit national values and win support of others through open media discourse and persuasion by the power of example. Methods of such persuasion may include positive comparisons between the self as an ideal and others as making progress toward matching that ideal.

However, when national confidence is lacking, the government tends to shift from a strategy of influence to the tools of propaganda, manipulation, and information war. The latter requires a considerable state effort to impose preferred frames and prioritize issues in news coverage. Such frames and priorities tend to reflect the emotions of fear and defensiveness—rather than a feeling of hope, as under the strategy of influence—presenting the "other" as uncooperative, lacking moral values, or even outright evil. Such strategies are commonly employed during international crises and wars. In those cases, the media work to emotionally discredit and dehumanize opponents by presenting them as deprived of any human values. For example, following the 2014 revolution in Ukraine, some Ukrainian officials and media called pro-Russian separatists "subhumans," while the Russian media referred to the new Ukrainian government as a "fascist junta."¹⁷ Overall, rather than expecting others to follow national values, the government actively promotes or defends them from possible attacks in the global media space. In such cases the state officials may perceive the world of global information in zero-sum terms and the "other" as a potential threat to national values.

Figure 2.1 summarizes the described international relationships, which are not limited to those among states but include media and society as historically continuous and relatively autonomous actors.

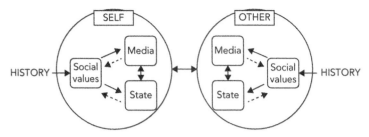

Figure 2.1 Values, Interstate Relations, and Media

American Fears of Russia

American fears of Russia have roots in the history and politics of interstate relations and media perception. Historically the two societies developed from different foundational beliefs about spiritual life, the economic and political system, and relations with the outside world.

The United States has viewed itself as the superior form of society, yet initially it did not seek to impose its model on others globally. The American founding fathers believed in the country's mission yet in Thomas Jefferson's expression of it: "This mission was not to intervene on every occasion to help oppressed people. Standing alone among the nations of the earth, she [America] could best fulfill this mission simply by existing and thus proving that self-government can succeed."[18] As with other growing and relatively isolated powers, the United States has operated from a deeply ethnocentric view of the world. Even though slavery in America was abolished only in 1865, it was Russia that was viewed as socially and politically oppressive.[19] Still, a distinction was made between the Russian political system and the national character of the Russian people, who were viewed as instinctively on the side of freedom and "far from being savage or even unamiable."[20]

At a later stage, guided by so-called Manifest Destiny, the US rulers established a regional hegemony expanding westward across the continent and creating a coherent state. Were Russia to stand in the way, Russophobic stereotypes could have emerged in the manner of those that America developed about China, Japan, Germany, and Muslim nations at later stages. But Russia was remote and caused no concerns. US officials were preoccupied with their own affairs and had few suspicions about the Russian empire. Unlike Europe, the United States produced no preeminent Russophobic writers, and "the trope of Russia as a giant octopus threatening to ensnare Europe had little currency in the United States until the Cold War."[21] The two nations viewed each other favorably during the American Revolution and throughout most of the eighteenth and nineteenth centuries, and they were allies during the world wars.

However, America's cultural lenses and the sense of distinctive national values and its "civilizing mission"[22] were bound to influence the country's foreign policy. In the early twentieth century, Theodore Roosevelt took the Japanese side in the Russo-Japanese War and said he would not mind "going to extremes" with the Russians.[23] Immigrant groups in the United States (especially Jews) began anti-Russian lobbing to "liberate" Russia from autocracy and anti-Semitism. American writers and journalists such as George Kennan assisted in popularizing antitsarist revolutionaries in the United States.[24] In 1911 the American government abrogated its commercial treaty with Russia.[25] In response to the Bolshevik revolution, the United States refused to recognize Soviet Russia from 1917 to 1933. Still, Russophobia rarely had a chance to principally influence the US foreign policy because Russia did not act as a challenging or globally threatening power.

This changed during the Cold War. Following World War II, the exceptional and originally isolationist vision of America as "one nation under God" and a "shining city upon a hill" took on the new meaning of being universally applicable in organizing human societies. While Soviet Russia made sense of the Cold War in terms of sovereignty and independence from Western pressures, the United States was working to promote the "universal" narrative of freedom and individual rights. American intellectuals, media, and politicians were craving "liberation" of Russia from the Soviet "oppression," while the US government worked to undermine the Kremlin's control of Eastern Europe and the Soviet Union.[26] In particular, a large amount of money was allocated for an aggressive anti-Soviet propaganda in the Western media. For the first time in history, defensive and globalist values clashed, defining the world until the Cold War's end. To both nations, the Cold War constituted a trauma that complicated their cooperation.

This complex and traumatic history posed problems for developing US-Russia relations following the Cold War. That the United States emerged in a position of dominance, whereas Russia was severely weakened, eventually exacerbated the trauma.

Initially, American fears of Russia were suppressed in expectation that the latter would transform its values in the manner of Western "democracy" and fight foreign threats alongside the United States. During the 1990s the American liberal media were not focused on Russia's corruption and abuses of power because the country's development was viewed as largely "transitioning" and conforming to standards of the West's political system.[27] The emotion of hope largely colored the American perception of Russia. After all, Russia recently ended the period of Communist rule that Ronald Reagan famously labeled "the evil empire." Similarly, US media provided relatively favorable coverage of Russia in response to the Kremlin's cooperation with the United

States following the terrorist attacks on the country on September 11, 2001.

However, by the middle of that decade, US media shifted to the discourse of fear, resuming the coverage of Russia and Putin as "evil" and "neo-Soviet." This shift occurred in response both to Russia's movement toward a more centralized system of authority less respectful of minority rights and to Russia's growing deviation from what the American media viewed as the appropriate value standard by which to assess others. Searching for the negative other in supporting the US-centered binary "freedom-oppression" narrative, the media found such an other in Russia.[28] Increasingly, Russia became associated with a dangerous autocratic system rooted in the Soviet political model. Russia was now commonly described in terms of its fitting with the old pattern. It was assessed not on the scale of how far it had gotten away from the Soviet system, but rather how far Russia had become a Soviet-like "one-party state" driven by a "KGB mentality" and dependent on the use of propaganda, "Cold War rhetoric," and repressions against internal opposition in order to consolidate state power.[29]

The activation of these fears became possible because of the dominance of liberal views in American political and media circles. Under the liberal narrative of globally marching "universal" democratic values promoted by the *New York Times*, *Washington Post*, *CNN*, and other networks, Russia's state consolidation and stress on order and sovereignty were viewed with suspicion. The media's dependence on a unifying narrative from which to cover foreign countries increasingly complicated US-Russia relations, and activities of special interest groups with anti-Russian agendas contributed to an increasingly hostile perception of Russia in mainstream media and political circles. Such perceptions betrayed a growing lack of confidence in the United States' ability to serve as the world's moral leader. According to sociologists, 2004 was the last year when public confidence in most institutions averaged better than 40%.[30]

The perception of Russia as the leading threat reached a new height following the revolution in Ukraine in February 2014 and election of Donald Trump as president of the United States in November 2016. Russia's annexation of Crimea and its support for separatists in the eastern part of Ukraine exacerbated fears of the Kremlin's "autocratic expansionism" and a drive to conquer Europe. Some writers in the *Washington Post* and the *New York Review of Books* went as far as to compare Russia's actions to those of Nazi Germany,[31] which incorporated Austria in 1938 before breaking up Czechoslovakia and igniting a world war. The implication was that the West must not appease an aggressive Russia and that only tough actions could stop it from further expansion. Leading American analysts of Russia such as Michael McFaul and Steven Sestanovich argued in *Foreign Affairs* that Russian foreign policy grew more aggressive in response to Putin's authoritarian politics, not US policies.[32]

During the US election campaign in 2016, liberal media frequently speculated that Putin wanted to bring his favored candidate, Trump, to power in order to then jointly rule the world. Trump was presented as an excessively pro-Russian candidate willingly or unwillingly undermining the United States' national security, whereas Russia was viewed as an offensive power aiming to undermine the US election system and even falsify the results of the presidential elections.[33] Following attacks on the Democratic National Committee and Wikileaks' release of confidential materials on Hillary Clinton, many in political and media circles concluded that the Kremlin had launched an information war on the United States with the purpose of destroying the democratic system in the country.[34]

The Role of Government

The influence of the US government on the media's perception of Russia has been essential. Despite autonomy and formal independence, the mainstream media frequently rely on the state for information. Through briefings, interviews, and articles by government officials, news writers and commentators may receive information not known to the public. While conveying such new information, the government also signals what it views as the appropriate tone and frames of coverage. Accordingly, the government is in a position to set the agenda and directly engage with the general public.

During the Cold War, the US government successfully influenced the agenda of various media and nongovernmental organizations to engage in fighting communism. For instance, organizations that had been created after World War II with an agenda of protecting global freedom and human rights, such as Freedom House and Human Rights Watch, were partly transformed into a tool for fighting the Soviets. Freedom House's slogan, "United States: country of freedom," removed all doubts about the nation's justified missionary objective to liberate the world and be free in choosing its means for undermining the "evil empire." The organization consistently abstained from criticizing the United States, choosing to instead direct attention outside.[35] As room for interstate dialogue shrank, the mainstream media also linked democracy and human rights agendas to those of defeating the Soviet Union.[36] As the Soviet side was fighting its own cultural Cold War via media and propaganda, the competition over international power increasingly defined perceptions of self and other. When pressured from outside, nations tend to react defensively by embracing ethnic prejudices, empowering nationalist voices, and engaging in exclusionary discourses of the other.

After the Cold War, the US state remained a major influence on the media by suppressing fears of Russia in times of cooperation and encouraging them during periods of interstate tensions. In the first years of the twenty-first century, the United States followed the strategy of influence with respect to Russia. The US media and policymakers were widely expecting Russia and other non-Western countries to become market democracies. The strategy of influence resulted from the world's generally high regard for American values and the US political class's confidence in the superiority of its system. The leading establishment journal, *Foreign Affairs*, summarized the dominant triumphal mood: "The Soviet system collapsed because of what it was, or more exactly, because of what it was not. The West 'won' because of what the democracies were—because they were free, prosperous and successful, because they did justice, or convincingly tried to do so."[37] The new Russian leaders themselves argued at the time that their country's "genuine" Western identity was hijacked by the Bolsheviks and the Soviet system. The dominant narrative was that the West's "victory" had sidelined those who believed that Russia presented a serious threat.

In the second half of the first decade of the century, and especially following reelection of Barack Obama as president, the government role in influencing media changed. By that time, the United States' global reputation had suffered, while Russia grew more powerful and assertive, aiming to further limit the West's global influence. In this environment, rather than discouraging the newly emerged narrative of Russia as a growing threat, the government sought to exploit it to its advantage. As the US media were shifting from the "hopeful transition" tone to that of castigating Russia as corrupt, autocratic, and illegitimate, the government was pressuring the Kremlin not to restrict the activities of the media and of foreign NGOs, while increasing financial assistance for domestic opponents of Putin. In response to Russia's propaganda and media attacks against Western values, members of the US political class and expert community began discussions of policies to counter the Kremlin's information campaign.[38]

The US government refrained from confrontational rhetoric, but made clear its highly critical view of Russia's political system, and it increased support for the country's pro-Western opposition. A 2007 report by the State Department condemned "centralization of power in the executive branch, a compliant State Duma, corruption and selectivity in enforcement of the law, media restrictions, and harassment of some NGOs," pledging various assistance to media and "democratic organizations" inside the country.[39] In 2006, the US government financed training for 2,700 broadcast journalists, and in 2007 it provided technical assistance for over 1,200 independent media outlets in Russia.[40]

The Kremlin's international assertiveness in the wake of the colored revolutions in the former Soviet region, intervention in Georgia in August 2008, practice of limiting space for political opposition, and annexation of Crimea provided a fresh context for viewing Russia as the leading threat to the West.

Obama's approach moved toward more assertive propaganda in response to the growing perception that Putin's return as president indeed made Russia a threat—an image that many within media and political circles had promoted since 2005. At the same time there emerged the view that more resources were needed to successfully promote Western values in the context of global media competition. In March 2011, while testifying to the Senate Appropriations Committee, Secretary of State Hillary Clinton called on lawmakers to abandon the US post–Cold War strategy in favor of a more Cold War–like propaganda and media strategy: "During the Cold War we did a great job in getting America's message out. After the Berlin Wall fell we said, 'Okay, fine, enough of that, we are done,' and unfortunately we are paying a big price for it. . . . Our private media cannot fill that gap. . . . We are in an information war and we are losing that war."⁴¹ Responding to the perceived threat of Russia's information power, the US government-controlled Broadcasting Board of Governors (BBG) sought to increase funding for Radio Free Europe / Radio Liberty to become more competitive with Moscow's Russia Today (RT), which is "generously funded, slick, and unconstrained by moral scruples."⁴²

Putin's return as president prompted new fears of Russia's propaganda, pressuring US officials to react. In March 2015, Secretary of State John Kerry said he was concerned the United States was falling behind when it comes to putting out information. He asked for additional funding to be provided for the BBG by stressing that RT's influence was growing worldwide and that the United States didn't have "an equivalent that can be heard in Russian."⁴³ In April 2015, California congressman and chairman of the House Committee on Foreign Relations Ed Royce and New York congressman Elliot Engel introduced the United States International Communications Reform Act. The day before the hearing, Royce published an op-ed in the *Wall Street Journal* titled "Countering Putin's Information Weapons of War," in which he wrote that Putin's information power "may be more dangerous than any military, because no artillery can stop their lies from spreading and undermining U.S. security interests in Europe."⁴⁴

Following the election of Trump as president, the US government was no longer speaking with the same voice. As the newly elected president signaled his intent to improve relations with Russia, some unidentified members of the government leaked transcripts of an intercepted conversation between General Michael Flynn and the Russian ambassador, Sergei Kislyak, to the *New York Times* and the *Washington Post*. The leak resulted in the resignation of Flynn from his recently assumed position of national

Table 2.1 US Values, Interstate Relations, and Media Views of Russia

	Values	Interstate relations	Media perception
1991–1995	Convergence	Cooperation	"Transition"
1995–2005	Growing divergence	Largely cooperation	"Chaos"
2005–2013	Consolidation of differences	Growing tensions	"Neo-Soviet autocracy"
2014–	Clash	Information war, sanctions	"Foreign enemy"

security advisor and energized discussion in the liberal media of Trump's possible collusion with a hostile power that seeks to undermine the United States' political system.[45]

A war of values returned and Russia, again, was its main front.

Table 2.1 provides a summary of the described developments. The next chapter analyzes in greater detail the US media perceptions of Russia after the Cold War.

3
American "Universal" Values and Russia

The perception of Russia by American media went through four distinct stages after the dissolution of the Soviet Union, each defined by the dynamics of the countries' respective values and interstate relations. As this perception moved through metaphors of "transition" from communism, "chaos," "neo-Soviet autocracy," and "foreign enemy," the two nations' value interaction became a cultural clash and interstate relations reached the stage of confrontation. Other factors that contributed to the increasingly negative perception of Russia by media included weak and opportunistic leadership, divisions within the US political class, the preferences of media editors, and the work of anti-Russian lobbies.

Russia in "Transition": The Early 1990s

Since the mid-twentieth century, the US media have played a key role in promoting what it viewed as the country's "universal" values of freedom and human rights. The Cold War divided the world in two parts, establishing a mirror image perception of each side's values. As told from the US perspective, the narrative of the Cold War was about American ideas of democracy as rescued from the threat of Soviet totalitarian communism. Although the media and politicians held different viewpoints over the methods of responding to the Soviet threat, they rarely questioned their underlying assumptions about national values and the morality of confronting the USSR. It therefore should not come as a surprise that many in the United States have interpreted the end of the Cold War as a victory for the Western narrative of values. Celebrating the Soviet Union's "grand failure,"[1] the American discourse assumed that thenceforward there would be little resistance to a worldwide progression of Western values. In the summary by Francis Fukuyama, the world lost any credible alternative system of values, as the end of the Cold War brought with it "the universalization of Western liberal democracy as the final form of human government."[2]

As a "defeated" power, Russia was widely expected to accept the new narrative of "universal" values. The West had proved itself to be morally superior and now had to teach the rest of the world about the "right" economic and political institutions. Russia's new leaders, at least initially, did not object to such a worldview, but it did not matter to the US media if they did or didn't. As American commentators were proclaiming the global spread of market democracy, Russia was viewed as an object, not subject, of the transformation. After all, in words of the *Wall Street Journal* and *Foreign Affairs*, there was now only "one dominant principle of legitimacy, democracy"[3] and only one dominant power to uphold this principle thanks to the superiority of its military, economic, and ideological capacity.[4]

In the early 1990s, Russia was a big story. The largest country on earth and the former enemy of the West was now led by radical pro-Western "reformers" who sought to rapidly transform Russia by turning it into a market democracy. The impatience for the transition from communism was everywhere, even in cartoons that served to demonstrate how the Russian masses were demanding a fast shift from their system to capitalism. For instance, a *Chicago Tribune* cartoon depicted a cleaning woman calling Russia's leaders from a Kremlin office and insisting that they "switch to a market economy *right now!!*"[5] This impatient attitude, along with the fear of Russia's reversal to the old days, also explains why the media were adamant that Yeltsin was the only true reformer and all those who opposed him were "hardliners" or "spoilers." When the democratic candidate Grigory Yavlinsky ran against Yeltsin during the 1996 presidential elections, the *New York Times* author Michal Specter wrote, "History will remember who was the spoiler if things go bad for democracy."[6]

Until the mid-1990s, the mainstream American media viewed Russia as generally on track in transitioning toward Western values. As Stephen Cohen writes, "Most journalists writing for influential American newspapers and news magazines believed in the Clinton administration crusade to remake post-Communist Russia."[7] During 1993–1994, in response to the failures of Russia's economic reforms and declining support for the Kremlin's pro-Western policies, some influential commentators began to question the wisdom of Russia's transition narrative.[8] Still, such views were a minority in the media and in policy circles. The majority was still advocating for a greater political and financial support for Russia's "democratic reformers."

The media's recommendations to the US government generally reflected a hopeful mood and aimed to strengthen Russia's president, Boris Yeltsin, as a radical pro-Western "reformer." American leadership was convinced that this was the only viable approach and promoted it in media and policy circles. Commentators rarely questioned US programs of economic assistance and efforts to discredit Yeltsin's political opponents. If anything, the media urged more assistance and a greater engagement with Russia in order for it to rapidly break with the Soviet past and embrace the West. Even when in October 1993 Yeltsin dissolved the parliament to rule by decree, most commentators applauded his actions. In December 1993, on the eve of a referendum on a new constitution that provided for a superpresidency and a weak parliament, the *New York Times* insisted that "Russia is moving convulsively to a new, more democratic political system."[9]

Russia in "Chaos": 1995–2005

In the second half of the 1990s, the transition narrative was increasingly replaced by that of "chaos" as Russia fought a devastating war in Chechnya, suffered from a financial collapse, and opposed NATO's bombing campaign in Yugoslavia. Russia was also hardly moving in the expected (Western) direction. Its economy was largely controlled by former high-ranking party and state officials with significant corruption and capital flight as inevitable consequences. The president had enormous power and could dissolve parliament and rule by decree.

Despite the continued support for Boris Yeltsin from the Clinton administration, by the spring of 1998 most journalists were deeply skeptical about Russia's transition and had developed a fatigue with it. For instance, in the summer of 1997 Hollywood released the hit *Air Force One* that portrayed Russia's president as a drunkard with no sense of direction who was unable to prevent the country's descent into crime, corruption, and ultimately ultranationalism.[10]

The media were now advocating a more cautious approach to Russia, calling for less assistance to "reforms." Among those challenging Western programs of engaging Russia and assisting it were former Cold War hawks such as William Safire and Zbigniew Brzezinski. Both questioned the idea of economic assistance, instead advocating for NATO expansion in preparation to confront Russia's "imperialist intentions" in the former Soviet region.[11] Most media were also increasingly critical of Yeltsin's policies with respect to Chechnya and domestic opponents. On Chechnya, American commentators embraced the decolonization argument, viewing Russia's problems in the Caucasus as a continuation of the imperial disintegration set in motion by Mikhail Gorbachev's reforms. Although President Bill Clinton defended the war in Chechnya by comparing it to the American Civil War,[12] most journalists viewed Russia's attempt to restore control in the Caucasus as both unjust and barbaric.[13]

Overall, the US media were now uncertain and divided on how to view Russia. The narrative of "universal" values suffered a major setback, yet the media had no replacement for it. Although no longer a threat, Russia was not moving in the expected "democratic" direction. Increasingly, it was viewed embroiled in chaos, yet—were the Kremlin to get its act together—democracy was there as a shining example.

The described uncertainty and divisions within political circles began to activate some old fears of Russia. Many in the West continued to mistrust the former "red menace," viewing it as threatening and barbaric. The growing post–Cold War divergence in values between the two countries was now framed as irreconcilable opposition. For instance, writing in *Foreign Affairs*, the historian Richard Pipes reminded readers about Russia's "heavy burden of history" and failure to make "a clean break with its Soviet past."[14] He cautioned against viewing the country as a potential ally and wrote that Russia could be back as an enemy if its leaders aspire to glory, rather than overcoming the legacy of communism, czars, and the Orthodox Church.

"Neo-Soviet Autocracy": 2005–2013

Beginning in roughly 2005, old fears increasingly came to shape the mainstream media perspective on Russia. The nation was "authoritarian at heart and expansionist by habit," as some commentators were already arguing in the 1990s.[15] This new perspective emerged in the context of Vladimir Putin's decision to oppose the United States' military intervention in Iraq, a series of steps to consolidate his domestic power, and an assertive foreign policy in Eurasia. The Kremlin opposed the Orange Revolution in Ukraine in November 2004 and intervened in Georgia in August 2008. The space for disagreement on Russia's direction narrowed, as the new highly critical view dominated the US media. Increasingly, Russia was viewed as a dangerous autocratic system with roots in the Soviet political model, oppressing its citizens and obstructing US-led globalization.

As is common in ethnocentric narratives, the neo-Soviet autocracy narrative was based on the image of an inferior Russia and a superior America. An example of such a binary presentation is the *Washington Post*'s explanation of the growing mistrust of the Kremlin in the United States:

> During the past decade, with former KGB officer Vladimir Putin in charge, Russia has become increasingly closed in many ways. Historical archives that after the collapse of the Soviet Union in 1991 welcomed scholars from all nations have reshut their doors. Television has fallen back under government control. International organizations have been pushed out of Russia, and independent nonprofit groups in Russia have been squeezed, harassed and threatened. Russia is essentially a one-party state, as it was 20 years ago.
>
> The United States by contrast is wide open. Unlike American organizations in Russia, the Russian government is welcome

to hire public relations firms here, put Russian programming on cable television and distribute its message as it sees fit. Its diplomats are welcome to attend think-tank seminars in Washington, and the give-and-take of American politics is an open book for them.[16]

Key frames here include characterizations of Russia as "closed" and associated with the KGB, the Soviet Union, and "government control," as well as the presentation of the United States as, "by contrast," "wide open," including to influences by the Russian government.

Analysis of editorials in three leading newspapers—the *New York Times*, the *Wall Street Journal*, and the *Washington Post*—provides a perspective on mass-media assessment of Russia during the indicated period (as summarized in figure 3.1). The three newspapers are representative of the mainstream perspective because they are the most widely read and capture a variety of audiences—the majority of Democrats and Republicans, politicians, members of business community, and the general public. While editorials may not be fully representative, they reflect the position of the newspapers' leadership and therefore constitute an important media sample. By explicitly stating views on various issues, editorials not only influence the audience, but also send important signals to staff reporters and potential authors in the opinion pages.[17]

The difference in perspective across newspapers was not significant, confirming a convergence of attitudes on Russia in the mainstream media. All three selected newspapers were overwhelmingly critical of Russia, with various degrees of intensity and emphasis on particular issues.[18] The media were initially softer on Dmitri Medvedev, who served as Russia's president during 2008–2011, with some expressing hope in his "capacity to reverse Russia's descent into authoritarianism and aggression,"[19] but soon were back to the highly critical attitude.

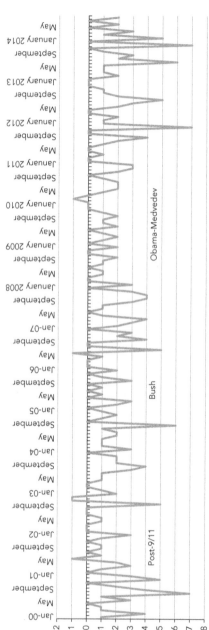

Figure 3.1 The US Media Perception of Russia, 2000–2014 *Source: Editorials on Russia in New York Times, Washington Post, Wall Street Journal*

'The texts for newspapers' editorials were obtained through the LexisNexis database. Only editorials on domestic issues including elections, opposition rights, rule of law, and others were selected, while editorials on foreign issues were excluded from the sample. The search resulted in 32 articles retrieved from *NYT*, 43 from *WSJ*, and 62 from *WP*, totaling 137 editorials. The retrieved articles were then read closely to identify main themes and media frames. The words were selected with the intent of capturing the emotions of hope and frustration as shaping Russia attitudes.

Each editorial was rated in terms of position on Russia's internal development. I coded as "positive" (+1) those articles that express hope for improvement and positive developments, as "negative" (−1) those that take a predominantly critical position, and as "neutral" (0) those that do not fit either one of these classifications. The analysis yields the combined score of the media's attitude toward Russia's internal development as negative across the identified period, with negativity figures ranging from 1 to 7. The score 0 captures either a neutral attitude or the absence of articles published during an indicated period.

Examples of the coding words for capturing the positive and negative tone of editorials and a fuller description of methodology of the textual analysis are provided in Tsygankov, "The Dark Double."

The identified periods reveal different frames through which the US media assessed Russia and its political system. Distinct frames and selected issues assisted the identified media in shifting to the neo-Soviet autocracy narrative. The media depiction can be presented in terms of three groups of issues—Russian internal politics, the attitude and power of Putin, and Russian foreign policy. For each issue, the narrative stressed some areas at the expense of others, and chose particular characterizations for the issues covered. Negative frames of state oppression were overwhelmingly dominant, whereas more positive or neutral ones, such as those stressing needs to address economic and security challenges, were never exploited.

By seeking to highlight the growing state control in Russia's political system, the identified US media advanced the image of Russia's political system as associated with the oppression of the opposition and minorities, fraudulent elections, indifference to the rule of law and the protection of citizens' property and security, and the systematic violation of individual rights. The assisting frames here include characterizations of the state that provoke negative emotions of fear and disrespect, highlighting its moral cynicism, reliance on force, and disregard for anything but the consolidation of power. The Russian state was one of "lawlessness and impunity" that exercises "brute force" in solving conflicts, "bullies domestic and foreign business," "systematically stifles" media and nongovernmental organizations, engages in aggressive disinformation, and uses crime and terrorism as an "excuse to further consolidate authoritarian control" and develop a "belligerent police state."[20]

By stressing Russia's "neo-Soviet" centralized control and abuses of power, the US media ignored areas of a relative autonomy and competition within the contemporary political system. For example, the internet, newspapers, and some radio and television channels (specifically Ekho Moskvy and Ren TV) were largely free of state control. Although the Kremlin restricted the activities of opposition leaders, some of them preserved the ability to challenge the authorities. For example, before the 2011 protests opposition leaders ran for the office of mayor in major cities. Many of those charged for disturbances during protests in early 2012 were either released or received sentences lighter than those expected. In December 2013, Putin also pardoned twenty thousand prisoners, including the members of Pussy Riot and his critic and former tycoon Mikhail Khodorkovsky. In February 2015, another Putin's critic, Alexei Navalny, was released from house arrest and formed a coalition to participate in new Duma elections.

Historical parallels in the identified US media also served to express feelings of fear, presenting Russia as a reinvention of the Soviet political system that functions as "a virtual one-party state," engages in "KGB-style" repressions, betrays Soviet-like "fear of competition," turns courts into "Stalinist show trials" against opposition, and resorts to a propaganda style worse than that during the Cold War.[21] Not only did the media make no distinction between Stalin-era and post-Stalin developments, but it also presented the Soviet experience as the only significant one for understanding Russia's historical trajectory. The tsarist system and its practices were rarely considered, although they may offer a different reading of Russia's political developments. The tsarist autocracy is not to be confused with totalitarianism or unlimited control over private and public life,[22] yet this is not what the editors of the *New York Times* or the *Washington Post* had in mind when they discussed Russia's "autocracy."

Similarly negative frames were advanced with respect to Putin as the architect of the "neo-Soviet" system. The characterizations used by the identified US media to describe Putin were also associated with the Soviet era: "KGB-trained," "like Stalin," and demonstrating a "conspiratorial KGB mentality."[23] The Putin persona was "paranoid and vindictive," "hyper aggressive" or "weak and insecure," "panicking"[24] with respect to his domestic and foreign opponents, or "hatemongering"[25] in exploiting Russian conservative attitudes toward gays. As to the system of governance established by Putin, it was described as "belligerent autocracy" and an "increasingly despotic one-man rule."[26] In this system, local leaders and successors were "hand-picked"[27] in order for the Kremlin to arrange and control all political developments.

The belief in Putin's omnipresence in Russian politics by the selected media was so powerful that they made no distinction between Putin and Russia's political class and society.[28] Putin was viewed as a ruler with dictatorial power similar to that of Stalin—responsible for all the achievements and flaws of Russia's political system—yet there was little appreciation of the state's administrative weakness and inability to deliver on its own promises. For instance, the US media rarely appreciated Russia's frequent ineffectiveness in dealing with serious problems, from mobilizing economic resources to solving crimes. More typically, the media designated Putin as responsible for the murders of journalists or opposition politicians, terrorist acts, and other grave developments in Russian politics. Thus, the mainstream media were united in holding Putin personally responsible for poisoning the FSB (Federal Security Service) defector Alexander Litvinenko, who shared state secrets with British intelligence.[29]

Even while presenting Putin's system as despotic and extreme in its degree of state control over society, the identified US media frequently assumed the system to be operating in a social vacuum. The *Wall Street Journal* expressed a common view in stating that a high level of public support for Putin predominantly resulted from the Kremlin's "relentless propaganda" and that, "when given a real democratic choice, millions of Russians will reject Putinism."[30]

Rather than discussing social sources of support for the state resulting from economic and political benefits brought by Putin's system or traditional pride in being a great power and a strong state, the media attributed such support to state repressions, propaganda, and diversionary foreign policy.

Finally, in covering foreign policy issues the newspapers relied on familiar Soviet frames, characterizing Russia's international behavior as excessively militaristic and cynical. In particular, the media described Russian foreign policy with terms such as "saber-rattling," "aggressive," and "threatening" in relations with the West,[31] and by characterizing such behavior as a "throwback to the Soviet times."[32] US newspapers further characterized Russia's official language as "Cold War rhetoric" and argued that the Kremlin exploited the image of an external enemy "as a scapegoat" for the purpose of suppressing domestic opposition. The *Washington Post* highlighted an "unusually strident" statement by President Medvedev in the context of describing the Kremlin's reaction to protests in Moscow following elections to the State Duma in December 2011.[33] In the statement the president warned that in response to US plans to deploy elements of a missile-defense system in Europe, Russia might aim its missiles at US installations on the continent and withdraw from the newly signed nuclear arms reduction treaty.

Table 3.1 summarizes the main media frames.

Value Differences and Interstate Tensions

Both value differences that became apparent after 2005 and growing interstate tensions contributed to the emergence of the neo-Soviet autocracy narrative in the media. Following the Orange Revolution in Ukraine, the Kremlin moved to formulate an alternative system of values based on conservatism, a strong state, and

Table 3.1 The US Media Frames of Russia

Issue	Frames	
	Characterization and metaphors	Historical parallels
Elections	"Potemkin elections"	"Soviet satellite regimes" "Virtual one-party state"
Opposition and minority rights	"Courageous" "Harassed and threatened" Murdered "critics of Putin" "Intolerance of homosexuality"	"KGB-style repression"
Justice system	"Lawlessness and impunity" "Rampant corruption" "Brute force"	Stalin's "show trials" "Czarist courts" Khodorkovsky as a "prisoner of conscience"
Business	"Bullying of domestic and foreign business"	Soviet-like "fear of competition"
NGOs, media, and civil society	"Systematically stifled" "Thuggery"	"Conspiratorial KGB mentality"
Terrorism & crime	"Excuse to consolidate" power "Domestic police state"	—
Governance	"Belligerent autocracy" "One-man show"	"Soviet political model"
Putin	"Paranoid and vindictive" "Weak and insecure" "Hatemongering"	"KGB-trained" "Like Stalin"
Medvedev	"Hand-picked" "Mini-me"	—
Foreign policy	"Authoritarianism and aggression" "Sabre-rattling" "Threat to the West" "Seeks a scapegoat"	"Throwback to the Soviet times" "Cold War rhetoric"

Source: Editorials on Russia in *New York Times*, *Washington Post*, and *Wall Street Journal*.

a multipolar balance of power. Russian society and the political class grew highly critical of American values and the notion of convergence with the West.³⁴ The US media saw these changes as threatening American values. Russia was too large and politically important to be ignored. In November 2005, the *Washington Post*, in its editorial "Mr. Putin's Counterrevolution," for the first time used the notion of autocracy in characterizing Russia's political system and argued against extending Putin the legitimacy of chairmanship within the Group of Eight.³⁵ Accustomed to covering Russia (and others) from the narrative of "universal" Western values, the media could not make sense of changes within Russia in any other way.

The relatively recent memory of the Cold War, a weak presidency, and activities of anti-Russian lobbyists helped to frame and consolidate the Russia-threat discourse in political and media circles. Despite considerable Russia cooperation following 9/11, talk of a new Cold War, with Russia as the main contributor, was increasingly popular as the decade progressed³⁶ and found support from some within the White House. The potentially promising path of US-Russia cooperation under George W. Bush was being subverted by those determined to present Russia as the leading threat to the West.

For instance, the influential vice president, Dick Cheney, accused Putin of reviving an authoritarian system and using its energy as a weapon of intimidation.³⁷ An experienced cold warrior, he was comfortable thinking about Russia as a potential threat and advocating what in practice would have amounted to a strategy of isolating Russia. After the Kremlin's attempts to influence the results of Ukrainian elections, the idea of confronting Russia by championing democratic values in the region became popular with both neoconservative and neoliberal thinkers and materialized in various publications and policy actions. In 2005 Freedom

House relegated Russia's ratings from "partially free" to "not free" (dictatorship), placing it next to Egypt, Rwanda, and Tajikistan and below Ethiopia and Libya.[38] Writing in the *New York Sun*, the Freedom House vice president argued that "Putin's Russia most closely resembles the Soviet Union of Leonid Brezhnev."[39] In 2006 a prominent report by the Council on Foreign Relations, *Russia's Wrong Direction*, formulated the idea of "de-democratization" or "rolling back democracy" by the Kremlin.[40] The two cochairs of the task force that produced the report argued in the pages of the *International Herald Tribune* that the Kremlin should be viewed as "illegitimate" by the United States.[41] Seeking to further undermine Bush's relations with Putin, Senator John McCain declared, "[When] I looked into Mr Putin's eyes I saw three things—a K and a G and a B."[42]

Many journalists sought to amplify the theme of internal repressions and anti-Western foreign policy by the "neo-Soviet" political regime. Fascination with Soviet KGB agents seizing power and turning the state into their own domain was strongly present in Western cultural products during the Cold War, and it continued to influence the writers of books about Russia, such as *Kremlin Rising* by Peter Baker and Susan Glasser.[43]

The image of Russia and its leadership turned largely negative after 2005. That image in the prominent US media did not change in a significant way despite the relative US-Russia rapprochement under President Dmitry Medvedev during 2008–2010. The period reflected hope associated with Barack Obama's attempt to "reset" relations with then-president Dmitri Medvedev and disappointment after 2011. Despite these differences, the media's assessment frequently failed to account for important changes between Medvedev's presidency and Putin's return. Rather, the media were generally uniform in assessing Russia negatively and applying the neo-Soviet narrative. Many analysts recognize that there are important differences between the two periods and that Russian politics incorporates a mixture of democratic and authoritarian characteristics,[44] although the space for radical criticisms within the country's political system narrowed in response to the return of Putin to the presidency in 2012 and the Ukraine crisis.

Overall, in the period 2005–2010, media and politicians increasingly displayed negative attitude toward Russia.[45] The debate on Russia was largely over, while the media's recommendations for the government were mostly in favor of isolating, containing, and confronting the country, while promoting NATO membership for Russia's neighboring countries. The neoconservative *Eurasia Daily Monitor* proposed that NATO be mobilized in response to the "energy threat" from the Kremlin and that Russia be treated as a militaristic anti-Western dictatorship and expelled from the G-8.[46] Writing in the *Hoover Digest*, Michael McFaul advocated adopting more sticks and fewer carrots toward Russia.[47]

The recommendations to isolate and punish Russia became especially loud after Putin's return to power in March 2012 and the crisis in Ukraine in 2014. Already under Medvedev, the mainstream US media had frequently advocated adopting "anticorruption" sanctions against Russia's prominent officials—a line of reasoning later developed and adopted in the so-called Magnitsky Law. Although the media were initially softer on Medvedev, many commentators were critical of attempts by the White House to improve relations with Russia's new president, arguing instead for strengthening ties with the "young democracies" Georgia and Ukraine and severing ties with the Kremlin.[48]

The new media consensus also meant that voices of dissent from the newly established perspective on Russia were increasingly sidelined. Criticisms of the US Russia policy and attempts to recognize the legitimacy of some of Russia's concerns in the mainstream media became rare and were frequently identified as apologies for the Kremlin. A case in point is the prominent scholar Stephen Cohen. Following new tensions in US-Russia relations, he remained critical of the dominant Western perception of Russia and continued to advocate restraint in foreign policy, focusing more extensively on the US side than on Russia.[49] As a result, multiple media sources such as the *New York Times*, the *New Republic*, state-funded Radio Free Europe / Radio Liberty, *Slate*, the *Weekly Standard*, and others published articles that branded Cohen an "apologist," a "useful idiot," and a "Putin's pal,"[50] while the scholarly Association for Slavic, East European, and Eurasian Studies at one time considered rejecting Cohen's philanthropic gift and denying him the right to establish a dissertation prize in his name.[51]

Until 2013, the US government was not receptive to the discourse of isolating and punishing Russia, instead advocating an interest-based dialogue with the Kremlin. George W. Bush continued his attempts to engage Russia until his departure. President Obama attempted to revive nuclear cooperation with Russia, proposing to "reset" relations with Medvedev and nurturing ties with pro-Western activists in Russia.

However, the US government too changed its view of Russia. Bush's and Obama's perception was that Russia was not a principal threat even though it was backtracking from democratic values. However, not yet perceived as a "threat," it was no longer "a nation in hopeful transition."[52] The White House's criticisms of Russia contributed to the media hostility that created a feedback loop of pressure on US officials. In the spring of 2012, influential media and political circles actively campaigned to prevent Obama from visiting Russia or developing contacts with Putin.[53] In 2013, a new campaign to sabotage Russia's Olympics in Sochi took place, as Obama came under renewed pressure to get tough with Putin.[54] In August 2013, *New York Times* columnist Thomas Friedman cited Putin's "abuse of Russian gays and lesbians, and his blatant use of rule-by-law tactics to silence any critics" as evidence that "we're not getting anything from this relationship anymore."⁵⁵ Another columnist, the former executive editor at the *Times*, Bill Keller, called Putin "a nationalistic and homophobic hard-liner" trying to start a new Cold War and "turn back 25 years of history."⁵⁶

Gradually and partly in response to media pressures, the perception of the Russian threat got consolidated within official circles. Responding to US-Russia clashes over the Magnitsky Law, Russia's laws against adoption of Russian children and "propaganda of non-traditional sexual relations,"⁵⁷ the handling of political protests by the Kremlin, and asylum for Snowden, the White House sought to exploit media pressure to influence Russia's domestic and international policies. In addition, the US government began to develop a new propaganda approach. Unlike the Cold War model, the new approach was proposed to be interactive or dialogue-based. Its purposes included repairing the damage to the US reputation from the WikiLeaks scandal, developing a more sophisticated understanding of the opposition in non-Western countries, and confronting potentially hostile non-Western regimes with new technology tools.⁵⁸

The US government also contributed to heightening the Russia threat by demanding additional resources needed to successfully promote Western values in the context of a global information war. In March 2011, while testifying to the Senate Appropriations Committee, Secretary of State Hillary Clinton declared, "We are in an information war and we are losing that war. Al Jazeera is winning, the Chinese have opened a global multi-language television network, the Russians have opened up an English-language network. I've seen it in a few countries, and it is quite instructive."⁵⁹ In October 2015, in her testimony on Ukraine before the Senate Foreign Relations Committee, Assistant Secretary Victoria Nuland raised alarms and called for actions to counter Russia's propaganda: "We must challenge the false narrative that nothing can or will change in Ukraine. To fight disinformation not only in Ukraine and Russia, but across Russian-speaking communities in Europe, we are joining forces with our partners in the EU to support alternatives to state-sponsored, Russian programming. We are also training foreign journalists and civil society actors in the art of fighting lies with the truth."[60]

Along with the development of the new propaganda approach, the United States engaged in various traditional forms of pressuring Russia. Along with European governments, it expressed strong criticism of the Kremlin's handling of political protests. In December 2012, the Congress passed the bill named after Russian accountant Sergei Magnitsky that imposed visa bans and asset freezes on human rights violators in Russia—long before Western sanctions were introduced against Russia in retaliation for the annexation of Crimea in March 2014. Here the media succeeded in its lobbying efforts—the law was eventually signed by President Obama. In July 2013 Obama canceled his summit in Moscow partly over Russia's decision to grant asylum to Edward Snowden, the NSA defector who made public surveillance activities by the US government of its citizens. The White House also launched an offensive on Russia's attempts to build a new union in Eurasia. Secretary of State Hillary Clinton's condemned the union as "re-Sovietization" in December 2012,[61] and the White House moved to support the Maidan Revolution and a change of power in Ukraine in February 2014, despite Russia's objection to what it viewed as an anticonstitutional coup. After Russia's intervention in Crimea and eastern Ukraine, the United States applied a broad range of sanctions against the Russian economy and limited bilateral and multilateral contacts with the Kremlin. Acting in sync with the media, in his 2014 State of the Union address, citing the Kremlin's actions in Ukraine, President Obama identified Russia as a leading threat to the world peace and the post–Cold War order, alongside the virus Ebola and the spread of terrorism in the Middle East.[62]

Despite attempts to build a sustained dialogue with foreign activists, a key thrust of the approach was still to activate propaganda, which the US government viewed as a vitally important, even indispensable foreign policy tool. As a result, the confrontational dimension in the approach played a key role. In practice, this meant a government integration of multiple public diplomacy and broadcasting agencies and the allocation of additional funds to confront potentially dangerous ideas in the global media space. On February 2, 2012, Director of National Intelligence James Clapper and CIA director David H. Petraeus stated in their testimonies to Congress that Russia and China pose significant security threats to the United States through their cyber and espionage activities and that Putin's return would make it more difficult to develop relations.[63] In 2014, Congress supported the effort by organizing hearings on propaganda and the information war and then introducing the United States International Communication Reform Act of 2014 to make the country's international broadcasting more effective in the face of state propaganda from Russia, China, Iran, and the Islamic State.[64]

"Foreign Enemy": 2014–2016

From around 2012 and especially since the Ukraine crisis in the early 2014, a new fear of Russia emerged and spread throughout the US media. In line with the old reasoning about autocracy's expansionism and disrespect for international rules,[65] the media viewed the Kremlin's annexation of Crimea and support for separatism in eastern Ukraine as evidence of preparations for a wider European offensive. Russia was also presented as launching an information war on the West with the purpose of destroying its values.

Since the Ukraine crisis, the US media have intensified their critique of Russia by focusing on its assistance to separatists in eastern Ukraine, military exercises on its border, and the propaganda campaign at home and abroad. The scapegoating I have already described was further developed with respect to Russia's Ukraine policy. As explained in a *Wall Street Journal* editorial, "Putin has complemented his aggressions abroad this year with a sharp crackdown against domestic opponents"[66] and integrated propaganda "with the Kremlin's model of ambiguous warfare, which relies on rapid action, covert troops, the creation of a digital fog of war, and inflaming ethnic and sectarian tensions."[67] Rarely did the US media mention the internal roots of Ukrainian instability, Russia's interests in the neighboring country, or threats to the legitimate government in Kiev by far-right groups.[68] The emphasis was, consistently with the narrative of autocratic expansionism, that Russia's "authoritarianism and aggression" went hand in hand.[69]

In order to stop Russia's "aggression," media recommended that the United States increase pressure on the Kremlin. For example, noting the crash of the ruble, the media attributed it to Putin's policies and proposed to increase the economic pressure on Russia by tightening sanctions in order to deter the Kremlin from potential external aggression.[70] The *Wall Street Journal* expressed fear that Putin might not be "accommodating in Ukraine or elsewhere" and called for supplying lethal arms for Ukraine's self-defense.[71]

Most commentators advocated a stronger response to Putin than that adopted by the White House, centered on sanctions against the Russian economy. Some, such as the president of the Brookings Institution, Strobe Talbott, proposed to return to a Cold War–like containment strategy, including arming Ukraine,[72] whereas others insisted on reviving an ideological struggle against Putin's "dictatorship."[73] The general hope expressed by the *Washington Post* was that Putin's regime was weak and that, despite his high poll numbers following the Crimea annexation, "the support is thin and unlikely to weather either a plummeting economy or substantial military casualties" that would follow from his support for eastern Ukraine.[74] Rather than discussing social sources of support for the state resulting from economic and political benefits brought by Putin's system or traditional pride in being a great power and a strong state,[75] the media attributed such support to state repressions, propaganda, and diversionary foreign policy.[76]

Russia's propaganda and information war became another object of Western media fears. The *Wall Street Journal* raised the alarm over the West's coverage of Russia Today, "Vladimir Putin's disinformation matrix" that framed Ukraine's prodemocracy uprising as a "Nazi" movement.[77] Although not effective in Western countries, the newspaper found RT propaganda to be achieving its objectives in "vulnerable states on Europe's eastern periphery and in the South Caucasus" and called on the West to respond by modernizing its public diplomacy.[78] Anne Applebaum and Edward Lucas frightened their readership with the system of "troll factories," which these columnists characterized as a much more powerful part of "Russia's disinformation empire" than RT.[79] In March 2014 former ambassador to Russia McFaul called for a new ideological confrontation with Putin's Russia.[80] Others insisted on the importance of fighting a "war of ideas,"[81] with the Heritage Foundation referring to the Kremlin as "an autocracy that justifies and sustains its hold on political power by force, fraud, and a thorough and strongly ideological assault on the West in general, and the U.S. in particular."[82] Peter Pomerantsev, coauthor of a report on Russian propaganda, testified before the House Foreign Affairs Committee in April 2014 that "Russia has launched the most amazing information warfare blitzkrieg we have ever seen."[83] In this climate even established American think tanks such as the

Carnegie Moscow Center became an object of attack as a "Trojan horse" for Putin's influence.[84]

In one sense Russian state propaganda was successful, that is, in terms of the results that the scare campaign brought in Washington. Chairman of the House Committee on Foreign Relations Ed Royce argued that the United States was on the defensive, as China, Russia, and Iran were more successful in leveraging information to their advantage. With respect to Russia, he raised special alarm: "Vladimir Putin has a secret army. It's an army of thousands of 'trolls,' TV anchors and others who work day and night spreading anti-American propaganda on the Internet, airwaves and newspapers throughout Russia and the world. Mr. Putin uses these misinformation warriors to destabilize his neighbors and control parts of Ukraine."[85] The main influences on Royce were writings by the Institute of Modern Russia, funded by the former oligarch Mikhail Khodorkovsky. One of its reports claimed that new technologies made Putin's Russia "arguably more dangerous than a communist superpower."[86] The scare campaign was effective, as evident in requests for additional funds for US government-controlled media. Broadcasting Board of Governors (BBG) member Leon Aron proposed to increase funding for Radio Free Europe / Radio Liberty, allowing it to become more competitive with Russia Today, which is "generously funded, slick, and unconstrained by moral scruples."[87]

In reality, Russia's state propaganda was not nearly so effective as it was painted, and is directed as much at the domestic audience as at the West. As Daniel Kennedy writes, "If there is an 'information war' being waged, it is an asymmetrical one, where Russia is at a disadvantage in the West."[88] Kennedy pointed out that, despite inflated claims by RT officials and those fearful of its informational power, RT's popularity on social media—judged by the number of followers of its Twitter account—is about one-tenth that of

BBC World News, let alone CNN. RT's performance on Facebook is better, yet one-fifth and one-eighth that of the BBC and CNN, respectively.[89] If one judges by funding, Russia is not in a very competitive position. The RT annual budget of $220 million compares poorly with the official budget of the BBG, which is over $721 million, in addition to an estimated $100 million in support from independent news publications' overseas and other programs within the US government.[90] Finally, the picture looks different if we judge by the popularity of Russia abroad. In the United States such popularity has declined considerably. For example, in March 2014, 68% viewed Russia as either an unfriendly or an enemy country, while favorable views of Putin were less than 10%.[91] These negative attitudes were recorded high since 1999.[92]

Conclusion

Overall, the US media coverage of Russia reflected American disappointment with Russia's failed transition to a more decentralized, Western-style system. Accustomed to the narrative of democratic transition, the media were at loss for new language to describe Russian affairs and soon turned to the familiar Cold War narrative of (neo-)Soviet autocracy and foreign threat. Two important contributing factors to consolidation of this narrative were growing interstate tensions between Russia and the West, and Russia's own strengthened state control and increasingly assertive foreign policy. The brief interlude of Dmitry Medvedev's presidency could not change the overall trend toward a hardening perception of Russia in American media and political circles. As a result, the US public grew critical of Russia's political system and became more receptive to references by the American establishment to Russia as a threat.

4
Russia Fights Back

This chapter addresses the frequently advanced argument that Russia itself is the reason the US media regard it as a threat. Many observers have asserted that the Kremlin depends on the image of foreign threat to consolidate its rule,[1] that state propaganda promotes anti-Americanism,[2] and that Russian foreign policy is unnecessarily confrontational and imperialist.[3] Russia therefore deserves to be criticized, and the Western media remain generally objective in their coverage of the country's politics.

The chapter argues that although Russia suffers from serious problems, these problems do not warrant the intensity of American media attacks on the country's political values, interests, and leadership. First, the media's perception of Russia as a neo-Soviet autocracy fails to understand the hybrid nature of the country's political system, which incorporates elements of legitimacy and democratic participation. Second, the US media pursue misleading historical parallels and omit from consideration similarities between contemporary Russia and its pre-Soviet or tsarist practices. Third, Western media's account is not self-reflective and does not notice the interactive dynamics between Russia's political practices and the West's own actions. At least some trends in Russia would have not progressed without Western pressures on the country. Thus the US media's tendency to focus the blame on Putin conceals that his policies often respond to actions by the United States. In the 1990s and early in the next decade, the Russians were quite receptive to American values but grew critical in response to US foreign policy.

Finally, Western media underestimate the level of genuine popular support for Putin and his policies inside Russia. For example, Russia's anti-Americanism remains popular not only because it is skillfully promoted in state-controlled media but also because of the cultural and political receptivity of the Russian general public. State propaganda is effective because it aims to discredit the United States' already unpopular policies and because it stresses values of independence that have been historically resilient in Russia.

Is Russia Blameless?

Russia's political system suffers from multiple problems. Revival of the state after the instability in the 1990s was essential for curbing the predatory instincts of the oligarchs, ending the war in Chechnya, improving living standards, and instilling a sense of stability and pride in the country's citizens. Under generally favorable international conditions, the state reversed the trend of disintegration and remained popular throughout most of the decade following. However, the end of the decade highlighted the Kremlin's inability to offer the country's citizens a model of stable economic growth and social welfare, a more open and legally transparent political system, an ideology inclusive of all ethnic groups, and an effective engagement with neighbors.

Russia's most important challenge in the twenty-first century remains that of development. Although largely successful relative to the fifteen years of decline (1990–2005),[4] Russia is only modestly successful relative to the rising challenges ahead. Russia has met some of its economic and security challenges, but it has also perpetuated an insufficiently diversified economic structure and weak social infrastructure. Government's promises notwithstanding, high oil prices slowed down its efforts to reduce reliance on energy exports. In terms of GDP, Russia's gap with developed nations is not likely to be narrowed in any meaningful way, and will continue to widen relative to China and India. Following the Ukraine crisis, the Russian economy has been negatively affected by the decline in oil prices and Western sanctions. As a result of these developments, in 2016 Russian per capita GDP had shrunk to the 2007 level, while the country's dollar-equivalent GDP was 40% below the 2013 level.[5] In terms of social development, Russia's human development index has yet to reach to the level of 1990, as is evident in the country's aging and declining population and deteriorating demographic indicators. These negative developments can only be reversed by massive state intervention and years of sustained economic growth.

Another serious problem is a relatively weak and administratively inefficient state. Formally Russia remains a strong state with large constitutional power vested in the president. However, in practice, the state is not sufficiently consolidated, lacking both the legitimacy and capacity to isolate the pressures of special interests.[6] As a result, it is frequently unable to deliver on its promises. The signs of paralysis are in political infighting within the Kremlin, corruption, and economic slowdown. Russian media sources report that only about 30% of presidential decrees are implemented.[7]

Russia's political system also lacks openness, transparency, and inclusiveness. Its political elites are frequently preoccupied with personal rewards and divided between those leaning toward the West and those advocating nationalist strategies. Russia is yet to establish institutions for reproducing an efficient and patriotic political class. Russia's elections are frequently falsified, while many social groups, including middle-class professionals, demand new channels for participation in politics and the emergence of institutions less dependent on personalities. The current State Duma has many loyalists to the Kremlin, a limited conservative opposition, and hardly any liberals. Russia's nationalists and probusiness interests are not represented politically. In the meantime, politicians and state media are often suspicious of people's aspirations and slow to recognize political criticisms and protests. For example, the protests on March 26, 2017, against Prime Minister Dmitri Medvedev's alleged corruption, in which some sixty thousand people participated, were not reported by state media, as if they never took place.

In foreign policy, Russia not infrequently relies on tough bargaining with neighboring states and cultivates relations with narrow elite groups. Perceived by many in the world as a corrupt power with the ruling class preoccupied with personal enrichment, Russia has problems with strengthening international relations. Some of the country's international actions are risky and potentially dangerous from the standpoint of human rights and the preservation of the regional balance of power.[8] The Kremlin is also known for a tendency to be paranoid about foreign threats, particularly those posed by the West.[9] Finally, the country's international assertiveness in relations with the European Union and the United States is often accompanied by an aggressive media campaign.[10]

The real issue is not whether Russia deserves to be criticized—all countries do—but the proportion, nuance, and political context of such criticism. Many media commentators in the West do not merely criticize Russia for abuses or ineffectiveness of power. Rather, they tend to perceive the very political and economic system of Russia as a fundamentally dysfunctional one that must be replaced by a Western-style competitive system. Because the Western system is "universal," any other system, by definition, is viewed as flawed.[11] Russia's system, in particular, is perceived as doomed to become a personalist rule that silences the voices of important population segments, deepens divisions within the ruling circles, engages in international adventurist behavior, and breeds future political crises.

However, this excessively critical perspective on Russia tends to exaggerate the nation's problems at the expense of its achievements. Presentations of Russia's problems as directly dependent on its "autocracy" not only simplify the country's challenges, but also misrepresent its political system. Russia's political system is not a liberal democracy or close to it. The system has been historically designed to meet challenges of ethnic diversity, economic development, and national security rather than those of individual freedom. This explains the difficulties of adjusting to the realities of spreading liberal democracy and globalization. Nevertheless, the system is far from being a dictatorship with no respect for citizens' rights.

Contemporary Russia is a system of limited, or "managed," democracy. There is a mix of democratic and authoritarian elements, which some Western scholars define as a hybrid or semiauthoritarian regime.[12] Although the system suffers from multiple problems concerning human rights and elections, there remains space for limited pluralism in Russia's political system, especially when compared to the Soviet period. Alternative news coverage remains available, as the internet, newspapers, and some radio and television channels are free of state control. There is also a limited space for political protests and the radical opposition's participation in national and local politics. The most prominent religious groups are able to operate relatively freely, and progress has been made in strengthening the rights of people with disabilities. The activities of opposition parties, alternative media, and the newly expanded Presidential Council for Civil Society and

Human Rights limit the ability of the regime to control opposition politics and indicate that the Russian state is, despite the very real concerns, not a dictatorship.

Most international ratings agencies, except Freedom House, recognize that Russia has a mixed form of political system. For example, Polity IV, affiliated with George Mason University, assesses countries on political competition and constraints on executive action. Scores range from −10 (fully institutionalized autocracy) to +10 (fully institutionalized democracy). Polity IV identifies a middle category, anocracy, which combines a mix of democratic and autocratic traits and practices, for scores ranging from −5 to +5. In the 2014 organization's report, Russia was listed as an open anocracy (In the 1–5 range), clustered in the group of countries below Western democracies but above China, Sudan, Egypt, and Kazakhstan.[13]

The US media's perspective on Russia suffers from ethnocentric and historic myopia. More often than not the media fail to provide a proper context for recognizing the country's distinct challenges. Historically, the country has had to master a vast open space with a harsh climate and resist strong threats from foreign invasion from the west and south. In addition, since the 1700s, Russia has been a semiperipheral country struggling to overcome its backwardness and lagging behind better-developed Western economies. Russia's system of a strong, concentrated state has had a mixed record, yet without it, it is hard to imagine the country preserving itself as a sovereign power and achieving its level of economic and technological development.[14]

Russia's system has also varied depending on the time and nature of its challenges. The parallels US media draw with Soviet (totalitarian) practices are misleading not only because they make no distinction between Stalin and post-Stalin developments, but also because they present the Soviet experience as the only significant one for understanding Russia's historical trajectory. If, however, the contemporary Russian system does not fit expectations of a Western-style democracy, this does not yet make this system a Soviet or neo-Soviet one. Instead, Russian analysts often reach back to its centuries-long political experience before communism and commonly resort to analogies of the times of trouble (*smuta*), dual power (*dvoyevlastiye*), in-between tsardom (*mezhdutsarstviye*), or other historically meaningful terms.[15] Although the US media make occasional references to "tsarist" practices, they are much more comfortable with the Soviet parallels—perhaps because they know too little of Russia's pre-Soviet history and its differences from the Soviet period. The inevitable unfortunate implication of the Soviet parallel is that the contemporary Russia's system is also suspected to be based on egregious level of violence similar to that during Stalin's era. In reality the post-Soviet system is based on a careful management of social and political tensions and of information, rather than violence.

The fact that some of Russia's systems and rulers have proven less effective is hardly an argument against more concentrated systems or strong states. All governments must balance citizens' demands for order and security with those of individual and group rights. Like other political systems, the strong state is an institutional arrangement to concentrate and distribute human resources in the interests of the common good. Some strong states have proven to be ineffective and prone to risky international behavior. Others, however, used their time wisely by capitalizing on the system's advantages, such as the ability to formulate long-term objectives and mobilize the required social and material resources.

Competitive or Western-style systems are also not always effective and suffer from multiple flaws. For instance, the media under liberal democracies frequently display tendency to be nonobjective and serve narrow special interests rather than the general public.[16]

Another problem is that Western systems often suffer from the nontransparent power of business lobbies and tend to function more like an oligarchy than a democracy. Western nations are often ruled by oligarchical elites on behalf of shrinking middle classes.[17]

Finally, it is misleading to present Russian foreign policy as autocracy-driven revisionism or expansionism. Not only does that portrait misrepresent the direction and scope of Russia's international actions, but it is frequently incorrect regarding the sources of such actions. Rather than being "expansionist" and "autocratic," Russian foreign policy is frequently defensive and defined by regional challenges and actions by Western powers.[18] A more realistic and nuanced approach to Russian foreign policy would begin by understanding the country's values, interests, and status aspirations. Such an approach would seek to establish meaningful historic, social, psychological, political, and military contexts in which Russia acts and seeks to achieve its goals. Finally, it would incorporate the level of power and confidence that provides the state with the required platform for acting, as well as the actions of the Western states toward Russia.

From Acceptance to Containment of American Values

Russian attitudes toward the United States and the perception of Russia evolved from an acceptance of Western values in the late 1980s and early 1990s to a growing resentment following 1993 and then rejection after 2007.

During the late 1980s, optimism and favorable attitudes toward the Western nations in general and the United States in particular prevailed. Inspired by Mikhail Gorbachev's ideas of perestroika, many Russians were increasingly supportive of the new stress on democracy, human rights, and transition away from the Soviet command economy. Within elite circles, an influential group emerged to push Gorbachev further toward an abandonment of socialism and state planning in favor of Western-style capitalism. It was this group's views that defined Russia's new foreign policy after Gorbachev's resignation in late 1991. With Francis Fukuyama, this group believed in Western-style liberal capitalism as the only system that is "normal" and "natural" for Russia to follow.[19]

The general public was supportive of the West and its values. In the early 1990s, Russians were especially interested in and attracted to the United States. Polls registered that of all nations in the world 39% of Russians expressed the strongest interest in America, relative to 27% interested in Japan and 17% in Germany.[20] When asked who should become Russia's favored partner, 74% chose the United State. As one pollster put it, "Unbelievable as it may seem, in the early 1990s the majority of Russian citizens viewed the United States not merely as the single superpower, but also as the unquestionable model to follow."[21] Media views reflected the growing recognition of Western values.

Opposition to such views was weak and expressed by Communist and radical nationalist newspapers and magazines such as *Den'*, *Nash sovremennik*, and *Sovetskaya Rossiya*. These media outlets typically portrayed the West as a collection of atomized individuals deprived of moral values and united only by aspirations to become rich at the expense of the rest of the world. A market economy and political democracy were presented as products of Western rationalist modernity that were unacceptable for Russia, with its search for the higher spiritual truth.[22]

The situation changed during 1992–1993, when most people began to withdraw their initial support for Western values. According to some polls, only 13% favored the US model of society in 1992.[23] Others pollsters found such support to be higher, but they too stressed the negative trend. For instance, in 1993 most people prioritized relations with the Commonwealth of Independent States (former Soviet states except the Baltics) (45%) over relations with the United States (35%), whereas in 1992 these priorities were reversed.[24] New concerns appeared. A 1995 poll revealed the growing fear that Russia was ceding its autonomy to the West in economic and other affairs. Among elites 44% and among the general population 75% believed that the economy was essentially in foreign hands.[25] The number of those viewing the West as seeking to weaken Russia also increased.

This growing resentment went through several stages and fluctuations, but continued to grow overall in response to Russia's negative experience with the West-supported economic reforms and disagreements on Yugoslavia (1999), Iraq (2003), and Georgia (2008).[26] In Yugoslavia, NATO, led by the United States, launched air strikes against Belgrade to stop the "ethnic cleansing" of Kosovo's Muslims. Russian liberals were especially worried about their country being pushed aside by the West. In his interview with Radio Free Europe / Radio Liberty, Yegor Gaidar, a radical liberal reformer and former prime minister, called NATO's campaign "the biggest error" of the alliance's existence and expressed fear of "very serious" consequences for Russian-US relations, possibly "the restoration of the Cold War . . . with a Russia that is afraid of the world, NATO, and America and that has missiles, a mobilized economy, and is friendly with authoritarian and rogue regimes."[27] In March 2003, the United States intervened in Iraq to remove Saddam Hussein, who was accused of developing nuclear weapons and maintaining relations with al-Qaeda. In August 2008, Western nations expressed their support for Georgia's president, Mikheil Saakashvili, who attacked the rebellious province of South Ossetia and found himself in a military conflict with Russia. In all these cases, most Russian media sources—even those generally sympathetic with the West—expressed their strong criticism of Western nations.

Around 2005, Russia's perception took another turn. Responding to the West-supported regime changes in the former Soviet region and the Middle East, the media began to reflect the government's search for indigenous Russian values distinct from those of West. Previously, since the mid-1990s, Russian media had been critical of the United States' foreign, but not domestic, politics. In particular, the media criticized what they viewed as the United States' "expansionism" and disregard for international law in response to the terrorist attacks of September 11, 2001.[28] The semiofficial *Mezhdunarodnaya zhizn'* noted that "under the slogan of the struggle with terrorism, the United States achieved an important geopolitical victory, especially in Central Asia and Caucasus—regions that Russia viewed in the area of its vital interests."[29] Others were concerned about negative domestic implications, including the radicalization of Russian Muslims and the rise of nondemocratic trends.[30] Now the difference in media coverage was that American foreign policy was scrutinized not only as a projection of power and economic interests, but also as a promotion of US-centered values. Even moderate and liberal newspapers such *Nezavisimaya gazeta* and *Kommersant* viewed the US strategy of promoting democracy as dangerous and as leading to greater instability and violations of human rights.

The overall coverage of US-Russia relations by Russian press has worsened since the second half of 2010. Even moderate Russian sources grew highly critical of the United States, though not at level of US media criticisms of Russia. Figure 4.1 summarizes Russian and American media perceptions of each other during 2008–2015, based on and analysis and rating of editorials published in *Nezavisimaya gazeta* (*NG*) and the *New York Times*.[31]

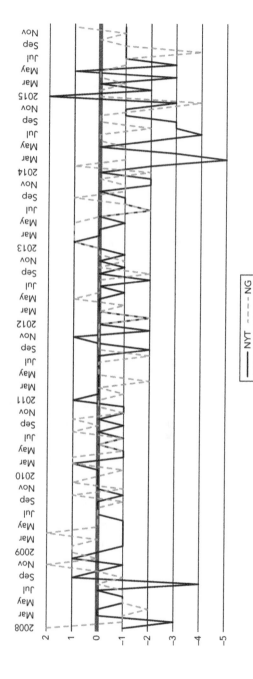

Figure 4.1 The US and Russian Media Perceptions of Each Other, 2008–2015
Source: Editorials on Russia in *New York Times*; editorials on the United States in *Nezavisimaya gazeta*.

The analysis captures that the United States was viewed more favorably in the identified Russian media during November 2008–October 2010 than previously and more negatively following October 2010. By comparison, the *New York Times* viewed Russia negatively throughout the whole period, although less so during Medvedev's presidency.

Based on qualitative analysis of frames in editorials published in *NG* during 2008–2015, the moderate Russian press sought to expose US foreign policy as a drive to expand American power and impose its values across the world. The newspaper's relevant editorials commonly referred to the US policy of promoting democracy as a cove for America's "geopolitical interests," as "propaganda," and as an attempt to establish new "spheres of influence."[32] Such a policy frequently meant "solidarity with an aggressor," as it was when the White House supported Georgia in its conflict with Russia despite President Mikheil Saakashvili's attacks against South Ossetia,[33] or a "violation of the United Nations' mandate," as happened when Western countries used the UN Security Council resolution authorizing air strikes against Libya to advance regime change there.[34] From the Russian media's perspective, the attitude of contempt for international law was also evident in the United States' treatment of individual cases, including those of Russian arms dealer Victor Bout, Julian Assange, and Edward Snowden.[35]

The *NG* viewed Western promotion of democracy as devoid of global legitimacy because the United States sought to "impose" its own "political model" in parts of the world where it would not be culturally sustainable.[36] As a result, West Europeans were deprived of their own voices and Middle Eastern countries experienced radicalization and civil war.[37] With respect to Russia and Ukraine, these policies revealed the United States' "prejudices and phobias" regarding attempts by Russia and its neighbors to build an economic union. In the words of one editorial, the

> Ukraine-centered confrontation is bipolar. On the one hand, there is Russia, on the other there is the West, especially the US. It is Washington that makes all the key decision on Ukraine—the government's head and composition, forms of assistance to Kiev, and types of sanctions against Moscow. . . . First and foremost, the purpose is to prevent restoration of the Soviet Union in any form. Fears of such revival take the form of prejudices and phobias. Any process of integration in the former Soviet space is condemned, whereas expressions of Russophobia are welcomed. Washington supports and assists the accession to power of local political elites that hold anti-Russian attitudes.[38]

As to sanctions and various forms of pressuring Russia politically, even the moderate *NG* speculated that such actions harbored the United States' intention to destroy the Russian economy, preserve dominance of the US dollar, and provoke mass political protests in the country, thereby fostering a resignation of Putin and regime change in the Kremlin.[39]

Adding the value dimension to covering US foreign policy also meant that Russian media were focusing on assessing the United States' internal political system and exposing perceived weaknesses of the American values that Washington was determined to promote abroad. Russian journalists and commentators criticized US elections, the institution of checks and balances, and economic injustice and ineffectiveness. One *NG* editorial characterized American presidential elections as a "battle of clans,"[40] an allusion to an oligarchical rather than democratic system. Other editorials critically assessed the US system's inability to restrain radical expressions of Islamophobia,[41] limit the power of specialized security agencies that spy on their own citizens,[42] promote a more egalitarian healthcare policy,[43] and overcome "political paralysis" between the executive and legislative branches of power over budgetary issues.[44] Finally, the Russian media criticized both the ineffectiveness and the design of an American "oligarchical" economic system that fostered inequality at home[45] and promoted global hegemony of the US dollar and multinational corporations.[46]

The more conservative and nationalist media in Russia, including the state-controlled TV and tabloids, presented the United States and the West in general as morally reprehensible for weakening traditional family and spiritual bonds and national unity. These values were largely shared by the generally conservative Russian public, but the choice by the media to present them in a binary opposition of moral versus immoral served the objective of strengthening national unity in the context of growing Western pressures.

The media defended traditional family values in Russia by attacking feminists, homosexuals, and the adoption of children by foreigners [47] State-controlled TV provided highly critical coverage of the punk band Pussy Riot. The three members of the group danced near the altar of Russia's main cathedral, calling on the Mother of God to "chase Putin away," and were eventually sentenced to two years of jail for hooliganism. Many Russians and Orthodox believers were offended by Pussy Riot's nonsanctioned performance, tight clothing, and incorrect way of crossing themselves. The fact that Western governments expressed strong disagreement with the verdict[48] only strengthened the polarizing presentation of the West as "immoral" by the media.

More extreme forms of media presentation included satirical TV footage of members of Pussy Riot having a sexual orgy in a public museum or one of them stealing a frozen chicken from a supermarket by putting it into her vagina.[49] Some media anchors proposed that homosexuality is a product of Satan and that "the

Table 4.1 The Russian Media Frames of the United States, 2007–2015

Issue	Justification and characterization
Democracy promotion	"Propaganda" and "geopolitical instrument"
NATO's purpose	Containing Russia and tying in Western European nations
Counterterrorism	"Myopic" and driven by narrow "political goals"
The Ukraine crisis	"Prejudices and phobias" of Eurasian integration
Sanctions against Russia	"Regime change" in the Kremlin
US elections	"Battle of clans"
US checks and balances	"Political paralysis"
US economic system	"Oligarchy" at home, "hegemony" abroad
Western cultural values	"Immoral"

Source: Editorials on the United States in *NG* and random articles in *Izvestia, Kommersant, Rossiyskaya gazeta*, and other media sources.

hearts of homosexuals should be burned and buried in earth because they're unsuitable for life."[50] In the meantime, social networks were actively spreading the meme of "Gayropa," in reference to the defense of gay rights in Europe. Russian media also actively opposed the adoption of children by foreigners and defended the law banning such adoptions by soliciting supporting opinions from experts and politicians. In his interview on the program *Odnako* on the TV channel Pervy Kanal, Sergei Markov stated that those opposing the law were acting on behalf of foreign interests—either they want to seize power in Russia in the interest of foreign states or they want Western money.[51]

Table 4.1 summarizes main frames concerning the United States as developed by the Russian media from 2007 to 2015.

Why Russia Is "Anti-American"

Russia's perception of the United States is similar to that of US views of Russia, in the sense that it reflects culturally distinct values exploited by media and state in the context of interstate tensions. However, Russia's perception is also shaped by state-media relations that are not present in the United States.

Historically, under the traditional tsarist and Soviet systems, the Russian state formally controlled media and information flow through the institution of censorship. Guided by a (quasi)religious ideology, Russia sought to preserve the principles it inherited from Byzantium in competition with the Catholic West. In line with these principles, ideology served to demonstrate a state-society unity in face of external pressures. The state therefore acted defensively on the perception of outside threats to Russia's identity. During periods of international crises, state-controlled media were principal actors in protecting national values from perceived encroachment by powerful Western states. Following the end of communism, the state no longer practices formal restrictions, but has developed various informal ways of shaping and influencing media. In part due to control of important TV channels and other types of media, the Russian state has retained a strong ability to obtain favorable media coverage and influence the public.[52]

When Russia entered the first period of tensions in relations with the West in the mid-1990s, the state was successful in reviving the defensive discourse of containing the external threat to national values. Initially, these values were defined as those of great-power status that Russia has historically sought to preserve. Here the state was able to utilize the experience with the Cold War during which the Soviet Union fought to preserve its independence from Western political and ideological pressures. Russians formulated the narrative of independence centuries ago, as they withstood external invasions from Napoleon to Hitler. The US decision to expand NATO and exclude Russia from the process played into the country's traditional fears, assisting the state with mobilizing opposition to the West. The decision strengthened the sense that

Russia was not being accepted by the Western nations, and it provided critics of cooperating with the United States and European countries with the required ammunition.

Having mobilized public opinion to oppose the West, the state was occasionally made vulnerable to media criticisms. For example, following the terrorist attacks on the United States on September 11, 2001, Putin proposed a strategic partnership with Washington on an antiterrorist platform, but many media outlets expressed criticism and mistrust of the West. The media reflected views of the Russian general public that, while supportive of Putin's leadership, showed signs of increased concern over American actions in the world. According to data from the Russian Center for the Study of Public Opinion, 63% of all Russians felt that the terrorist attack on the United States was a form of "retribution for American foreign policy."[53] Even progovernment media were concerned with the Kremlin's growing support for US global policies.[54]

Another critically important turn came around 2005. Responding to colored revolutions in Eurasia and fears of regime change, the Kremlin began to articulate a new system of internal values as distinct from those of the West. At first, the stress was on the importance of preserving sovereignty in building Russia's own political system, which the Kremlin defined as democracy at its own pace. In his speech delivered to the Federation Council in March 2005, Putin warned against attempts to destabilize Russia's political system by "any unlawful methods of struggle" and insisted on moving toward values of freedom and democracy at Russia's own pace.[55] The deputy head of the presidential administration, Vladislav Surkov, rationalized the idea by introducing the theory of "sovereign democracy," which meant to protect Russia's internally determined path of development.[56] In practice, the theory of distinct values meant that the Kremlin begun to train its own youth organizations, restrict the activities of Western NGOs and radical opposition inside the country,⁵⁷ and signal to the media the importance of promoting Russia's sovereign values and discrediting those of the West. By this time the state had already assumed control over public TV, stripping powerful media tycoons such as Boris Berezovski and Vladimir Gusinski of their economic empires.

The new turn in framing values signaled language and historical parallels supportive of the official discourse. Surkov's writings were widely discussed in Russian media, with many commentators citing approvingly the notion of a state-protected system of values.⁵⁸ Russian media also praised the Kremlin's steps to control the historic narrative. In particular, in June 2009 Medvedev announced the establishment of a commission to monitor and counter "attempts to falsify historical facts and events" that might undermine Russia's "international prestige."⁵⁹ In particular, the Russia's leadership sought to capitalize on the victory over Nazi Germany, stressing Russia's great-power status and playing down the Soviet occupation of Eastern Europe.⁶⁰

Another major shift in framing Russia's values took place following Putin's return to the presidency in March 2012. Beginning with his election campaign, Putin promoted a vision of Russia as a culturally distinct power, committed to defending values different from those of the West and other civilizations. In multiple statements, he criticized what he saw as Europe's departure from traditional religious and family values. In his Valdai Club speech, Putin quoted Russian traditionalist thinkers and declared "the desire for independence and sovereignty in spiritual, ideological, and foreign policy spheres" as an "integral part of our national character."⁶¹ In his 2013 address to the Federation Council, he further positioned Russia as a "conservative" power and the worldwide defender of traditional values.⁶² Inside the country, Putin stressed the importance of strengthening traditional family values and articulating a new idea uniting Russians and non-Russian nationalities. The

Kremlin presented such idea as that of state-civilization with a special role historically played by ethnic Russians identified as "the core (*sterzhen'*) that binds the fabric" of the country's culture.[63] The discourse of distinctiveness grew stronger in the context of the Ukraine crisis. In particular, Putin sought to justify the incorporation of Crimea in terms of consolidating Russia's civilizational values on imperial grounds. In his speech on Crimea, Putin presented it as "an inseparable part of Russia" and a foundation of its civilizational values, a place in which Prince Vladimir, who christened Rus' in the Orthodox faith, had been christened himself.[64]

The distinctive feature of this stage of Russia's containment of Western values was that the Kremlin could no longer be satisfied with defensive and internal steps, but increasingly took the fight to the West's media space. In order to protect Russia's "spiritual sovereignty," Moscow also began to advocate its own version of soft power and information management. In July 2012, in his meeting with Russia's ambassadors Putin urged them to actively influence international relations by relying on the tools of lobbying and soft power.[65] The Kremlin established an infrastructure to influence the formation of Russia's image in the world. The Russia Today television network soon became an TV- and internet-based outlet to promote Russia's worldview globally. Several state-supported foundations and the Russian Orthodox Church actively promoted linguistic and spiritual relations to Russia across the post-Soviet region. In 2012 the state also instituted Rossotrudichestvo (Russian Cooperation) as the organization through which to connect to those with ties to Russia in Eurasia by distributing foreign aid and creating "optimal conditions for promoting Russian business, science, education, and culture."[66]

Following the Ukraine crisis, the Russian state became especially alarmed by a perceived expansion of Western values and sought to prevent it by tightening control over domestic media and information space. During 2014–2015, state-controlled media were predominantly focused on developments in Ukraine, presenting those as a confrontation between values of the "Russian world" and those of Russophobic descendants of the Nazis backed by the West.[67] According to Putin, Western nations were behind the revolutionary change of power in Kiev without understanding their destabilizing consequences. In justifying his intervention in Crimea, Russia's president said that he acted on behalf of the overthrown but still legitimate president of Ukraine, Victor Yanukovich, and that the action was necessary to prevent violence and the violation of human rights in the region by the "rampage of Nazi, nationalist, and anti-Semitic forces."[68] In addition to tightening control over state-owned TV channels and newspapers, the Kremlin found ways to shape and frame discussions on the internet.[69]

The success of state efforts reflected not only novel ways to frame national values in opposition to the West and the material resources allocated for propaganda purposes, but also the traditionally influential values of the strong state. The country's tradition of a powerful executive had centuries-long roots predating the Soviet and even tsarist systems. Despite various criticisms of Russia's autocratic system as prone to dictatorship, most Russian rulers viewed the institution as essential for supporting popular aspirations, overcoming partisanship, and protecting Russia from outside interferences. The unusually strong support for Putin reflects not only resentment toward perceived Western pressures on Russia, but also respect for the idea of a strong state that the president embodies. Putin is the central part of a leader-centered political system and the architect of its contemporary version. When the US media are critical of him, they are also critical of the Russian system of values—to be more precise, of a particular presentation and personification of these values. In a system that some observers describe as "illiberal democracy,"⁷⁰ Putin's popularity is also a reflection of national perceptions. The Kremlin's propaganda is effective in part because it stresses historically resilient traditional values in Russia.⁷¹

Indeed, the Russian view of democracy is distinct in the sense that it avoids oppositions between "order" and "rights," instead favoring their combination. When asked whether it is possible for Russia both to be democratic and to have a strong state, more than 50% Russians believe that they can have both.⁷² The belief in a strong state is likely to be behind the view that Russia needs its own unique type of democracy, established on the basis of national traditions and distinct from the democracies of European or Soviet type. From the second half of the first decade of the century to the early 2010s, such a view was shared by 45% to 50% of the respondents, and that figure declined to below 40% only at the height of the economic decline in response to the global financial crisis. On the other hand, those advocating Western-style democracy were 20%–25% of respondents, while those arguing for the Soviet system could muster support of about 15%.⁷³

The first post-Soviet leaders did not mean to radically break with the country's traditionally strong executive branch. Even Yeltsin, who in the Western media is typically viewed as the father of Russia's democracy and market economy, demonstrated the intent to revive the tradition of a strong state. He supported the new constitution in which presidential power was expansive and had few checks and balances, he used force in Chechnya, he attempted to discipline oligarchs by unleashing his security services on them, and he issued some tough warnings to the West.⁷⁴ It was Yeltsin who selected the West-critical Yevgeny Primakov as the second foreign minister and Putin as his successor. Putin's acceptance of democracy and a market economy was itself conditioned on the recovering capabilities of a strong Russian state. Answering a question about Chechnya and human rights, Putin stressed that "if by democracy one means the dissolution of the state, then we do not need such democracy."[75] By seeking to strengthen the state, Putin built the system in which political competition and media freedom are restricted by the authorities' perspective of what is necessary for preserving internal stability during a time of economic transition and reforms.

The discourse of Russia's distinctiveness as accentuated by the conflict with the West was highlighted during the country's presidential election in March 2018. The official results—77% support for Putin and the turnout of 67%—exceeded the expectations of many observers. Although the results were contested, analysts recognize that the overall message was that most Russians trust Putin, even if many of them favor more attention to economic development.[76] Arguing against the *Washington Post*'s dismissal of the election's results as a sham, Timothy Frye noted that "the Kremlin continues to benefit from the annexation of Crimea, the stabilization of the economy, and the resurgence of Russia on the global stage."[77] Two other scholars concluded that Russians felt better about their president and the country despite four years of declining living standards and that "the ensuing conflict with Ukraine and the West did wonders for Putin's popularity, boosting his approval numbers from the mid-60s to the mid-80s."[78]

The contribution of Western pressures to Putin's success was significant. Sanctions by the United States and the EU against Russian officials and the country's economy and accusations of Moscow's meddling in Western elections and poisoning of independent journalists and defectors abroad were the context for Russia's elections. Immediately before the election, Great Britain ordered twenty-three Russian diplomats to leave the country and accused Moscow of poisoning the former Russian intelligence officer Sergei Skrypal. The Kremlin's tough response to Britain by the Kremlin and its indignation over the British accusation mobilized popular anger over disrespectful treatment by Britain.⁷⁹ By supporting Putin, Russians voted not just for the president, but for a commander in chief who is capable of protecting the country from Western pressures and unfounded accusations.

5
Russophobia in the Age of Donald Trump

This chapter addresses the new development in the US media perception of the Russian threat following the election of Donald Trump as the United States' president. The election revealed that US national values could no longer be viewed as predominantly liberal and favoring the global promotion of democracy, as supported by Presidents Bill Clinton, George W. Bush, and Barack Obama. During and after the election, the liberal media sought to present Moscow as not only favoring Trump but being responsible for his election and even ruling on behalf of the Kremlin. Those committed to a liberal worldview led the way in criticizing Russia and Putin for assaulting liberal democratic values globally and inside the United States. This chapter argues that the Russia issue became so central in the new internal divide because it reflects both political partisanship and the growing division between the values of Trump voters and those of the liberal establishment. The domestic political struggle has exacerbated the divide. Russia's otherness, again, has highlighted values of "freedom," seeking to preserve the confidence of the liberal self.

The Narrative of Trump's "Collusion" with Russia

During the US presidential election campaign, American media developed yet another perception of Russia as reflected in the narrative of Trump's collusion with the Kremlin.[1] Having originated in liberal media and building on the previous perceptions of neo-Soviet autocracy and foreign threat, the new perception of Russia was that of the enemy that won the war against the United States. By electing the Kremlin's favored candidate, America was defeated by Russia. As a CNN columnist wrote, "The Russians really are here, infiltrating every corner of the country, with the single goal of disrupting the American way of life."[2] The two assumptions behind the new media narrative were that Putin was an enemy and that Trump was compromised by Putin. The inevitable conclusion was that Trump could not be a patriot and potentially was a traitor prepared to act against US interests.

The new narrative was assisted by the fact that Trump presented a radically different perspective on Russia than Clinton and the US establishment. The American political class had been in agreement that Russia displayed an aggressive foreign policy seeking to destroy the US-centered international order. Influential politicians, both Republicans and Democrats, commonly referred to Russian president Putin as an extremely dangerous KGB spy with no soul. Instead, Trump saw Russia's international interests as not fundamentally different from America's. He advocated that the United States to find a way to align its policies and priorities in defeating terrorism in the Middle East—a goal that Russia shared—with the Kremlin's. Trump promised to form new alliances to "unite the civilized world against Radical Islamic Terrorism" and to eradicate it "completely from the face of the Earth."[3] He hinted that he was prepared to revisit the thorny issues of Western sanctions against the Russian economy and the recognition of Crimea as a part of Russia. Trump never commented on Russia's political system but expressed his admiration for Putin's leadership and high level of domestic support.[4]

Capitalizing on the difference between Trump's views and those of the Democratic Party nominee, Hillary Clinton, the liberal media referred to Trump as the Kremlin-compromised candidate. Commentators and columnists with the *New York Times*, such as Paul Krugman, referred to Trump as the "Siberian" candidate.[5] Commentators and pundits, including those with academic and political credentials, developed the theory that the United States was under attack. The former ambassador to Russia, Michael McFaul, wrote in the *Washington Post* that Russia had attacked "our sovereignty" and continued to "watch us do nothing" because of the partisan divide. He compared the Kremlin's actions with Pearl Harbor or 9/11 and warned that Russia was likely to perform repeat assaults in 2018 and 2020.[6] The historian Timothy Snyder went further, comparing the election of Trump to a loss of war, which Snyder said was the basic aim of the enemy. Writing in the *New York Daily News*, he asserted, "We no longer need to wonder what it would be like to lose a war on our own territory. We just lost one to Russia, and the consequence was the election of Donald Trump."[7]

The election of Trump prompted the liberal media to discuss Russia-related fears. The leading theory was that Trump would now compromise America's interests and rule the country on behalf of Putin. Thomas Friedman of the *New York Times* called for actions against Russia and praised "patriotic" Republican senators John McCain and Lindsey Graham for being tough on Trump.[8] MSNBC host Rachel Maddow asked whether Trump was actually under Putin's control. Citing Trump's views and his associates' travel to Moscow, she told viewers, "We are also starting to see what may be signs of continuing [Russian] influence in our country, not just during the campaign but during the administration—basically, signs of what could be a continuing operation."[9] Another *New York Times* columnist, Nicholas Kristof, published a column titled "There's a Smell of Treason in the Air," arguing that the FBI's investigation of the Trump presidential campaign's collusion "with a foreign power so as to win an election" was an investigation of whether such collusion "would amount to treason."[10] Responding to Trump's statement that his phone was tapped during the election campaign, the *Washington Post* columnist Anne Applebaum tweeted that "Trump's insane 'GCHQ tapped my phone' theory came from . . . Moscow." McFaul and many others then endorsed and retweeted the message.[11]

To many within the US media, Trump's lack of interest in promoting global institutions and his publicly expressed doubts that the Kremlin was behind cyberattacks on the Democratic National Committee (DNC) served to exacerbate the problem. Several intelligence leaks to the press and investigations by Congress and the FBI contributed to the image of a president who was not motivated by US interests. The US intelligence report on Russia's alleged hacking of the US electoral system released on January 8, 2017, served to consolidate the image of Russia as an enemy. Leaks to the press have continued throughout Trump's presidency. Someone in the administration informed the press that Trump called Putin to congratulate him on his victory in elections on March 18, 2018, despite Trump's advisers' warning against making such a call.[12]

In the meantime, investigations of Trump's alleged "collusion" with Russia were failing to produce substantive evidence. Facts that some associates of Trump sought to meet or met with members of Russia's government did not lead to evidence of sustained contacts or collaboration. It was not proven that the Kremlin's "black dossier" on Trump compiled by British intelligence officer

Christopher Steele and leaked to CNN was truthful. Russian activity on American social networks such as Facebook and Twitter was not found to be conclusive in determining outcomes of the elections.[13] In February 2018, a year after launching investigation, Special Counsel Robert Mueller indicted thirteen Russian nationals for allegedly interfering in the US 2016 presidential elections, yet their connection to Putin or Trump was not established. On March 12, 2018, Senate Intelligence Committee chairman Richard Burr stated that he had not yet seen any evidence of collusion.[14] Representative Mike Conaway, the Republican leading the Russia investigation, announced the end of the committee's probe of Russian meddling in the election.[15]

Trump was also not acting toward Russia in the way the US media expected. His views largely reflected those of the military and national security establishment and disappointed some of his supporters.[16] The US National Security Strategy and new Defense Strategy presented Russia as a leading security threat, alongside China, Iran, and North Korea. The president made it clear that he wanted to engage in tough bargaining with Russia by insisting on American terms.[17] Instead of improving ties with Russia, let alone acting on behalf of the Kremlin, Trump contributed to new crises in bilateral relations that had to do with the two sides' principally different perceptions. While the Kremlin expected Washington to normalize relations, the United States assumed Russia's weakness and expected it to comply with Washington's priorities regarding the Middle East, Ukraine, and Afghanistan and nuclear and cyber issues.[18] Trump also authorized the largest expulsion of Russian diplomats in US history and ordered several missile strikes against Assad's Russia-supported positions in Syria, each time provoking a crisis in relations with Moscow. Even Secretary of State Rex Tillerson, whom Rachel Maddow suspected of being appointed on Putin's advice to "weaken" the State Department and "bleed out" the FBI,[19] was replaced by John Bolton. The latter's foreign policy reputation was that of a hawk, including on Russia.[20]

Responding to these developments, the media focused on fears of being attacked by the Kremlin and on Trump not doing enough to protect the country. These fears went beyond the alleged cyber interference in the US presidential elections and included infiltration of American media and social networks and attacks on congressional elections and the country's most sensitive infrastructure, such as electric grids, water-processing plants, banking networks, and transportation facilities. In order to prevent such developments, media commentators and editorial writers recommended additional pressures on the Kremlin and counteroffensive operations.[21] One commentator recommended, as the best defense from Russia's plans to interfere with another election in the United States, launching a cyberattack on Russia's own presidential elections in March 2018, to "disrupt the stability of Vladimir Putin's regime."[22] A *New York Times* editorial summarized the mood by challenging President Trump to confront Russia further: "If Mr. Trump isn't Mr. Putin's lackey, it's past time for him to prove it."[23] The burden of proof was now on Trump's shoulders.

Opposition to the "Collusion" Narrative

In contrast to highly critical views of Russia in the dominant media, conservative, libertarian, and progressive sources offered different assessments. Initially, opposition to the collusion narrative came from the alternative media, yet gradually—in response to scant evidence of Trump's collusion—it incorporated voices within the mainstream.

The conservative media did not support the view that Russia "stole" elections and presented Trump as a patriot who wanted to make America great rather than develop "cozy" relationships with the Kremlin. Writing in the *American Interest*, Walter Russell Mead argued that Trump aimed to demonstrate the United States' superiority by capitalizing on its military and technological advantages. He did not sound like a Russian mole. Challenging the liberal media, the author called for "an intellectually solvent and emotionally stable press" and wrote that "if President Trump really is a Putin pawn, his foreign policy will start looking much more like Barack Obama's."[24] Instead of viewing Trump as compromised by the Kremlin, sources such *Breitbart* and *Fox News* attributed the blame to the deep state, "the complex of bureaucrats, technocrats, and plutocrats," including the intelligence agencies, that seeks to "derail, or at least to de-legitimize, the Trump presidency" by engaging in accusations and smear campaigns.[25]

Echoing Trump's own views, some conservatives expressed their admiration for Putin as a dynamic leader superior to Obama. In particular, they praised Putin for his ability to defend Russia's "traditional values" and great-power status.[26] Neoconservative and paleoconservative publications like the *National Review*, the *Weekly Standard, Human Events Online*, and others critiqued Obama's "feckless foreign policy," characterized by "fruitless accommodationism," contrasting it with Putin's skilled and calculative geopolitical "game of chess."[27] A Washington Post / ABC News poll revealed that among Republicans, 75% approved of Trump's approach on Russia relative; 40% of all respondents approved.[28] This did not mean that conservatives and Republicans were "infiltrated" by the Kremlin. Mutual Russian and American conservative influences were limited and nonstructured.[29] The approval of Putin as a leader by American conservatives meant that they shared a certain commonality of ideas and were equally critical of liberal media and globalization.[30]

Progressive and libertarian media also did not support the narrative of collusion. Gary Leupp at *CounterPunch* found the narrative to be serving the purpose of reviving and even intensifying "Cold War-era Russophobia," with Russia being an "adversary" "only in that it opposes the expansion of NATO, especially to include Ukraine and Georgia."[31] Justin Raimondo at Antiwar.com questioned the narrative by pointing to Russia's bellicose rhetoric in response to Trump's actions.[32] Glenn Greenwald and Zaid Jilani at *Intercept* reminded readers that, overall, Trump proved to be far more confrontational toward Russia than Obama, thereby endangering America.[33] In particular Trump weakened diplomatic ties with Russia, armed Ukraine, appointed anti-Russia hawks, such as ambassador to the United Nations Nikki Haley, National Security Advisor John Bolton, and Secretary of State Michal Pompeo to key foreign policy positions, antagonized Russia's Iranian allies, and imposed tough sanctions against Russian business with ties to the Kremlin.[34]

The dominant liberal media ignored opposing perspectives or presented them as compromised by Russia. For instance, in amplifying the view that Putin "stole" the elections, the *Washington Post* sought to discredit alternative sources of news and commentaries as infiltrated by the Kremlin's propaganda. On November 24, 2016, the newspaper published an interview with the executive director of a new website, PropOrNot, who preferred to remain anonymous, and claimed that the Russian government circulated pro-Trump articles before the election. Without providing evidence on explaining its methodology, the group identified more than two hundred websites that published or echoed Russian propaganda, including WikiLeaks and the *Drudge Report*, left-wing websites such as *CounterPunch, Truthout, Black Agenda Report, Truthdig*, and *Naked Capitalism*, as well as libertarian venues such as Antiwar.com and the Ron Paul Institute.[35] Another mainstream liberal outlet, CNN, warned the American people to be vigilant against the Kremlin's alleged efforts to spread propaganda: "Enormous numbers of

Americans are not only failing to fight back, they are also unwitting collaborators—reading, retweeting, sharing and reacting to Russian propaganda and provocations every day."[36]

However, voices of dissent were now heard even in the mainstream media. Masha Gessen of the *New Yorker* said that Trump's tweet about Robert Mueller's indictments and Moscow's "laughing its ass off" was "unusually (perhaps accidentally) accurate."[37] She pointed out that Russians of all ideological convictions "are remarkably united in finding the American obsession with Russian meddling to be ridiculous."[38] The editor of the influential *Politico*, Blake Hounshell, confessed that he was a Russiagate skeptic because even though "Trump was all too happy to collude with Putin," Mueller's team never found a "smoking gun."[39] In reviewing the book on Russia's role in the 2016 election *Russian Roulette*, veteran *New York Times* reporter Steven Lee Myers noted that the Kremlin's meddling "simply exploited the vulgarity already plaguing American political campaigns" and that the veracity of many accusations remained unclear.[40]

Explaining Russophobia

The high-intensity Russophobia within the American media, overblown even by the standards of previous threat narratives, could no longer be explained by differences in national values or by bilateral tensions. The new fear of Russia also reflected domestic political polarization and growing national unease over America's identity and future direction.

The narrative of collusion in the media was symptomatic of America's declining confidence in its own values. Until the intervention in Iraq in 2004, optimism and a sense of confidence prevailed in American social attitudes, having survived even the terrorist attack on the United States on September 11, 2001. The country's economy was growing and its position in the world was not challenged. However, the disastrous war in Iraq, the global financial crisis of 2008, and Russia's intervention in Georgia in August 2008 changed that. US leadership could no longer inspire the same respect, and a growing number of countries viewed it as a threat to world peace.[41] Internally, the United States was increasingly divided. Following presidential elections in November 2016, 77% of Americans perceived their country as "greatly divided on the most important values."[42] The value divide had been expressed in partisanship and political polarization long before the 2016 presidential elections.[43] The Russia issue deepened this divide. According to a poll taken in October 2017, 63% of Democrats, but just 38% of Republicans, viewed "Russia's power and influence" as a major threat to the well-being of the United States.[44]

During the US 2016 presidential elections, Russia emerged as a convenient way to accentuate differences between Democratic and Republican candidates, which in previous elections were never as pronounced or defining. The new elections deepened the partisan divide because of extreme differences between the two main candidates, particularly on Russia. Donald Trump positioned himself as a radical populist promising to transform US foreign policy and "drain the swamp" in Washington. His position on Russia seemed unusual because, by election time, the Kremlin had challenged the United States' position in the world by annexing Crimea, supporting Ukrainian separatism, and possibly hacking the DNC site.

The Russian issue assisted Clinton in stressing her differences from Trump. Soon after it became known that DNC servers were hacked, she embraced the view that Russia was behind the cyberattacks. She accused Russia of "trying to wreak havoc" in the United States and threatened retaliation.[45] In his turn, Trump used Russia to challenge Clinton's commitment to national security and ability to serve as commander in chief. In particular, he drew public attention to the FBI investigation into Clinton's use of a private server for professional correspondence, and even noted sarcastically that the Russians should find thirty thousand missing emails belonging to her. The latter was interpreted by many in liberal media and political circles as a sign of Trump's being unpatriotic.[46] Clinton capitalized on this interpretation. She referred to the issue of hacking as the most important one throughout the campaign and challenged Trump to agree with assessments of intelligence agencies that cyberattacks were ordered by the Kremlin. She questioned Trump's commitments to US national security and accused him of being a "puppet" for President Putin.[47] Following Trump's victory, Clinton told donors that her loss should be partly attributed to Putin and the election hacks directed by him.[48]

Clinton's arguments fitted with the overall narrative embraced by the mainstream media since roughly 2005 characterizing Russia as abusive and aggressive. Clinton viewed Russia as an oppressive autocratic power that was aggressive abroad to compensate for domestic weaknesses. Previously, in her book *Hard Choices*, then-secretary of state Clinton described Putin as "thin-skinned and autocratic, resenting criticism and eventually cracking down on dissent and debate."[49] This view was shared by President Obama, who publicly referred to Russia as a "regional power that is threatening some of its immediate neighbors not out of strength but out of weakness."[50] During the election's campaign, Clinton argued that the United States should challenge Russia by imposing a no-fly zone in Syria with the objective of removing Assad from power, strengthening sanctions against the Russian economy, and providing lethal weapons to Ukraine in order to contain the potential threat of Russia's military invasion.

Following the elections, the partisan divide deepened, with liberal establishment attacking the "unpatriotic" Trump. Having lost the election, Clinton partly attributed Trump's victory to the role of Russia and advocated an investigation into Trump's ties to Russia. In February 2017 the Clinton-influenced Center for American Progress brought on a former State Department official to run a new Moscow Project.[51] As acknowledged by the *New Yorker*, members of the Clinton inner circle believed that the Obama administration deliberately downplayed DNC hacking by the Kremlin. "We understand the bind they were in," one of Clinton's senior advisers said. "But what if Barack Obama had gone to the Oval Office, or the East Room of the White House, and said, 'I'm speaking to you tonight to inform you that the United States is under attack . . .' A large majority of Americans would have sat up and taken notice . . . it is bewildering—it is baffling—it is hard to make sense of why this was not a five-alarm fire in the White House."[52]

In addition to Clinton, many other members of the Washington establishment, including some Republicans, spread the narrative of Russia "attacking" America. Republican politicians who viewed Clinton's defeat and the hacking attacks in military terms included those of chairman of the Senate Armed Services Committee John McCain, who stated, "When you attack a country, it's an act of war,"[53] and former vice president Dick Cheney, who called Russia's alleged interference in the US election "a very serious effort made by Mr. Putin" that "in some quarters that would be considered an act of war."[54] A number of Democrats also engaged in the rhetoric of war, likening the Russian "attack," as Senator Ben Cardin did, to a "political Pearl Harbor."[55]

Rumors and leaks, possibly by members of US intelligence agencies,[56] and activities of liberal groups that sought to discredit Trump contributed to the Russophobia. In addition to the DNC hacking accusations, many fears of Russia in the media were based on the assumption that contacts, let alone cooperation with the

Kremlin, was unpatriotic and implied potentially "compromising" behavior: praise of Putin as a leader, possible business dealings with Russian "oligarchs," and meetings with Russian officials such Ambassador Sergei Kislyak.[57]

There were therefore two sides to the Russia story in the US liberal media—rational and emotional. The rational side had to do with calculations by Clinton-affiliated circles and anti-Russian groups pooling their resources to undermine Trump and his plans to improve relations with Russia. Among others, these resources included dominance within the liberal media and leaks by the intelligence community. The emotional side was revealed by the liberal elites' values and ability to promote fears of Russia within the US political class and the general public. Popular emotions of fear and frustration with Russia already existed in the public space due to the old Cold War memories, as well as disturbing post–Cold War developments that included wars in Chechnya, Georgia, and Ukraine. In part because of these memories, factions such as those associated with Clinton were successful in evoking in the public liberal mind what historian Richard Hofstadter called the "paranoid style" or "the sense of heated exaggeration, suspiciousness, and conspiratorial fantasy."[58] Mobilized by liberal media to pressure Trump, these emotions became an independent factor in the political struggle inside Washington. The public display of fear and frustration with Russia and Trump could only be sustained by a constant supply of new "suspicious" developments and intense discussion by the media.

Russia's Role and Motives

Russia's "attacking" America and Trump's "colluding" with the Kremlin remained poorly substantiated. Taken together, the DNC hacking, Trump's and Putin's mutual praise, and Trump associates' contacts with Russian officials implied Kremlin infiltration of the United States' internal politics. Yet viewed separately, each was questionable and unproven. Some of these points could have also been made about Hillary Clinton, who had ties to Russian—not to mention Saudi Arabian—business circles and Ukrainian politicians.[59] Political views cannot be counted as evidence. Contacts with Russian officials could have been legitimate exchanges of views about two countries' interests and potential cooperation. Even the CIA- and the FBI-endorsed conclusion that Russia attacked the DNC servers was questioned by some observers on the grounds that forensic evidence was lacking and that it relied too much on findings by one cybersecurity company.[60] In general, discussion of Russia in the US media lacked nuances and a sense of proportion. As Jesse Walker, an editor at *Reason* magazine and author of *The United States of Paranoia*, pointed out,

> There's a difference between thinking that Moscow may have hacked the Democratic National Committee and thinking that Moscow actually hacked the election, between thinking the president may have Russian conflicts of interest and thinking he's a Russian puppet . . . when someone like the New York Times columnist Paul Krugman declares that Putin "installed" Donald Trump as president, he's moving out of the realm of plausible plots and into the world of fantasy. Similarly, Clinton's warning that Trump could be Putin's "puppet" leaped from an imaginable idea, that Putin wanted to help her rival, to the much more dubious notion that Putin thought he could control the impulsive Trump. (Trump barely seems capable of controlling himself.)[61]

The loose and politically tendentious nature of discussions, circulation of questionable leaks and dossiers complied by unidentified individuals, and lack of serious evidence led a number of observers to conclude that the Russia story was more about stopping Trump than about Russia. The Russian scandal was symptomatic of the poisonous state of bilateral relations that Democrats exploited for the purpose of derailing Trump. US-Russia relations became a hostage of partisan domestic politics. As one liberal and tough critic of Putin wrote, Democratic lawmakers' rhetoric of war in connection with the 2016 elections "places Republicans—who often characterize themselves as more hawkish on Russia and defense—in a bind as they try to defend to the new administration's strategy towards Moscow."[62] Another observer noted that Russiagate performed "a critical function for Trump's political foes," allowing "them to oppose Trump while obscuring key areas where they either share his priorities or have no viable alternative."[63]

The described lack of confidence was reflected in the exaggerated fear that Russia was capable of destroying the West's values. However, Russia and Putin were neither omnipresent nor threatening to destroy the United States' political system. A number of analysts, such as Mark Schrad, identified fears of Russia as "increasingly hysterical fantasies" and argued that Russia was not a global menace.[64] If the Kremlin was indeed behind the cyberattacks, it was not for the reasons commonly broached. Rather than trying to subvert the US system, it sought to defend its own system against what it perceived as a US policy of changing regimes and meddling in Russia's internal affairs. The United States has a long history of covert activities in foreign countries.[65] Washington's establishment has never followed the advice given by prominent American statesmen such as George Kennan to let Russians "be Russians" and "work out their internal problems in their own manner."[66] Instead, the United States assumes that America defines the rules and boundaries of proper behavior in international politics, while others must simply follow the rules.

Russia's basic motives remain defensive even when the Kremlin relies on assertive tactics. Russia's assertiveness, even in cyberspace, is of a reactive nature and is a response to US policies. Experts observe that Russia's conception of cyber and other informational power serves the overall purpose of protecting national sovereignty from encroachments by the United States.[67] Rather than fighting a full-scale information war with the West, Russia seeks to increase its status and strengthen its bargaining position in relations with the United States.[68] The Kremlin has been proposing to negotiate rules of cooperation in the cyber area since early in the twenty-first century. Motivated by an insistence on "cyber-sovereignty," Russia regularly proposes resolutions at the United Nations to prohibit "information aggression," In a 2011 letter to the United Nations General Assembly, Russia proposed an "International Code of Conduct for Information Security," stipulating that states subscribing to the code would pledge to "not use information and communications technologies and other information and communications networks to interfere with the internal affairs of other states or with the aim of undermining their political, economic and social stability."[69]

Overall, what the Kremlin challenges is the United States' post–Cold War behavior that undermines Russia's status as a great power. Although Russia is not in a position to directly challenge the United States and the US-centered international order, the Kremlin hopes to gain external recognition as a great power by relying on low-cost methods and revealing the vulnerability of Western nations. Russia's capabilities and presence in global cyber and media space are limited, and the Kremlin is motivated by asymmetric deployment of its media, information, and cyber power.

6
Conclusion

The chapter summarizes the book's argument and reflects on future clashes of values in US-Russia relations. I argue that cultural and political divides come from different sources, but in times of acute competition between states, culture and politics reinforce each other in exacerbating international tensions.

American Values and Russia

This book has examined US-Russia relations in the realm of values. From the era of great hopes and expectations in the early 1990s, the two nations moved toward resentment and then further toward an emotionally bitter conflict of values. Since at least 2012, it has become common to hear American and Russian media accusing leaders of the opposing sides not only of violating international law, but also of developing political systems that are based on cynicism, injustice, and disregard for human dignity. On many occasions, US officials and members of the political class used the inflammatory rhetoric of comparing President Putin's actions with those of the Nazi leader Adolf Hitler and portraying the Kremlin's style of government as deeply corrupt and based on repression of the opposition, rewarding political cronies, and military invasions abroad. The Kremlin has reciprocated by exploiting anti-Americanism to stabilize the regime and by attacking the US practices of *diktat* (dictating) abroad and corruption at home. Comments by Russian officials reveal that they do not hold in high regard the American institutions of competitive elections, free media, and a market economy. Rather, they believe that such institutions serve as a cover for narrowly based yet excessively powerful special interest groups.[1]

The US media have not been helpful in fostering a spirit of objectivity and patient US-Russia cooperation. Rather than serving as a platform for a dialogue, the media have reinforced prejudices and stereotypes dominant in mainstream political circles. In this book, I have offered evidence that over the last fifteen years or so, the American media have circulated overwhelmingly negative images of Russia as an autocratic, abusive, and revisionist power. A more recent narrative presented it as involved in "collusion" with Trump for the purpose of waging a war on the United States and its values of individual freedom. Putin has been demonized as personally responsible for hacking the US elections, ordering the murders of defectors to the West, and covering up chemical weapons attacks by Syria's regime. In the media's perception, Russia "violates the most elemental norms of international behavior"[2] and therefore must be rolled back by striking "at the foundations of Mr. Putin's regime" and imposing additional sanctions, asset freezes, and visa bans on prominent officials and entrepreneurs.[3]

The media in Russia have also relied on disparaging characterizations of the US political system, particularly since 2012, favoring negative frames over more neutral and positive ones. For instance, rather than stressing American achievements, Russian journalists frequently presented the United States as a nation in decline and under growing pressures at home.[4] This negative image was briefly softened following the election of Trump, before Russia's hopes for improving ties with America dissipated.[5] However, in the late spring of 2017 Russian media resumed their highly critical coverage of the United States' domestic and foreign policy. Russia's TV and newspaper commentators often present American politicians as incapable of dialogue and driven to preserve the United States' global domination at any human cost. Being thoroughly disappointed in Trump, Russian media frequently attack him as someone who is prepared to launch a war on Russia. While some in the Russian media present him as internally weak and dependent on the "deep state" for his own survival, others view Trump as reckless and itching for a global confrontation with Russia to demonstrate America's power.[6]

Overall, the analysis of US and Russian media confirms scholarly conclusions about the media's importance in shaping a nation's political and cultural identity. Through the rejection of difference, the binary "self versus other" assists a country in maintaining its moral and psychological confidence. Both American and Russian media commonly offered one-sided interpretations of complex processes, exploited misleading historical analogies, and ignored areas of development that did not fit their favored narratives of the other. The US narrative about a threatening neo-Soviet autocracy has been instrumental in confirming the identity of America as free at home and as the leader of the "free world" abroad. The narrative assists the media in engaging with the US public in part because old Cold War views have not disappeared from the public mind and have not been replaced by a different understanding of new realities. Following the election of Trump as president, the liberal media presented him as acting on the Kremlin's behalf in defeating the liberal candidate, Hillary Clinton. Russia's otherness, again, distracted public attention from failed liberal policies and preserved the confidence of the liberal self. As Anatol Lieven wrote, "Whipping up fear of Russia allows elites in both the USA and Europe to continue to structure their institutions and strategies around an adversary that is familiar, comfortable and fundamentally safe."[7] Partly as a result of media presentations of the country, only 25% of Americans had a favorable opinion of Russia in March 2018—the highest negative since the Cold War—while the number of those disliking Russia reached 72%.[8]

On the other hand, the Russian media narrative about a globally intrusive, dictatorial, and internally corrupt America serves to worsen Russians' opinion of the United States and to strengthen Russia's identity as an independent great power guided by superior values and principles. Presenting the promotion of democracy and human rights as inseparable from the United States' hegemonic ambitions helps the Kremlin to rally supporters for its policies inside and outside Russia.[9] In the age of global information competition, the media, more than ever, serve to articulate and consolidate national symbols and emotions.

Is Russia Doomed to Be the Dark Double?

The described clash of values in US-Russia relations was hardly inevitable in the sense that alternative strategies and ideas existed in both countries. Influential intellectuals, organizations, and members of the political class voiced their support for cooperation based on mutual interests in fighting terrorism, regional instability, and weapons proliferation. Yet each time, those advocating exclusive values, rather than inclusive solutions, prevailed.[10] As I argued, this happened through a combination of two factors: perception of the other side's recognition of the self's values and interests; and the self's internal confidence in its ability to promote or sustain its values. The United States shifted toward negative presentation of

Russia in response to perceived challenges to its interests and values globally, including challenges from Russia. The Kremlin's value strategy was more regional and local, resulting from perceived Western pressures and internal confidence. Driven by such perceptions, ruling elites postponed searches for cooperation and adopted policies of unilateral protection of each side's interests.

The identified value conflicts had roots in both cultural and political divides. Against some initial expectations, the age of globalization has not replaced the world of nation-states, but rather introduced new conditions, in which national identities, values, and institutions express themselves by reviving some old, historically established ideas and practices. As one American commentator wrote, it is abundantly clear that many in the West "underestimated the role of nationalism and other forms of local identity, including sectarianism, ethnicity, tribal bonds, and the like. . . . [I]t turns out that many people in many places care more about national identities, historic enmities, territorial symbols, and traditional cultural values than they care about 'freedom' as liberals define it."[11]

US-Russia conflicts have roots in history and politics. Due to the history of Cold War and some earlier developments, the United States and Russia built principally different political institutions. After the Cold War, the two nations did not view each other as adversaries, and their leaders rarely used the emotional and mutually alienating language of exclusive values until the early 2010s, or some twenty years later. However, during this time, the two nations failed to bridge the old cultural gap—largely because of existing and increasingly diverging political expectations. While Washington expected Russia to accept the United States' new status as the only superpower, the Kremlin never relinquished hopes to recover as a global power after the Cold War and expected the White House to respect Russia's claims of equality. It was only a matter of time before these radically different, indeed irreconcilable expectations would clash, pushing the two countries toward rivalry, including in the realm of values.

The US media led the way in creating the narrative of threatening neo-Soviet Russia before American government officials chose to exploit it. Although the United States' public did not hold an overwhelmingly negative image of Russia, public perception became more critical after the late 1990s, creating a space for reviving the neo-Soviet, neo–Cold War narrative by the mainstream media. In developing the narrative, the media were arguably less influenced by the public than by various groups with anti-Russian feelings and preferences within the US political class. These groups were suspicious of Putin's arrival as president of Russia, and by the middle of the first decade of the new century, they widely publicized their view of the country's deviation from the "right path." In the eyes of the mainstream liberal media, Russia's diversion from building a Western-style political system and cooperating with the West in foreign policy "confirmed" these groups' assessments. The mainstream media then faithfully reflected the new perception of Russia by the public and especially by the elites.

Governments played an especially prominent role in developing and consolidating these negative perceptions. By the mid-2000s, US leadership began to rely on such a perception, as George W. Bush's statements during the Bratislava "democracy" summit made clear. However, Bush and subsequently Obama refrained from using the inflammatory language that later became common in the media, and each hoped to find an understanding with Putin on the basis of US priorities. In the meantime, the Kremlin was frightened by the Washington's strategy of global regime change and the colored revolutions in Eurasia, and was increasingly skeptical that mutual understanding was possible.

These two divergent perceptions doomed the period of Obama-Medvedev cooperation to failure and then clashed following Putin's return as president in 2012. At this point, the divergent political perceptions reinforced the growing cultural divide. First, the United States and then Russia deployed the emotional language of value confrontation in attempting to pressure the other side politically. US leadership sought to keep Russia's political system open to American economic and political interests, whereas the Kremlin wanted guarantees against foreign "intervention." Both sides developed media strategies—assertive from the Washington and defensive from Moscow—in order to promote or sustain their internal political values. The United States has moved away from trying to win hearts and minds by developing "digital" and financial tools for engaging foreign activists and monitoring foreign governments. Activities of the US government exposed by Julian Assange and Edward Snowden indicated that the power of example was being replaced with that of assertiveness, surveillance, and bribery in defeating the US opponents. In its turn, the Kremlin tightened political control over digital and media spaces out of fear of Western encroachment on Russia's sovereignty.

As E. H. Carr wrote, state power is prepared to go far to exploit and create "the morality convenient to itself."[12] Before the end of the Cold War, the United States already had such a morality system established as a "market democracy." During the Cold War, the idea of market democracy obtained the status of ideology, fighting on behalf of freedom against the totalitarian communism.[13] As far as Russia is concerned, it abandoned its Soviet system of values only to discover the older historical pattern of a strong state. The latter was gradually revived in response to pressures from the West. Observers documented how the Kremlin improvised and experimented with different strategies of opposing Western influences,[14] yet it is equally important to identify similarities between the newly introduced "morality" and the tsarist practices of state dominance in the areas of information, politics, and economics. As previously in its history, Russia's system of values developed in tension with and in response to that of Western nations. Ideas of Christianity, communism, and liberal democracy all had their roots in the West, yet each was adapted to fit Russia's own geopolitical and domestic conditions. Ironically, instead of transforming Russia's traditional institutions, Western pressures contributed to these institutions' revival.

Following the election of Trump the US media's perception of Russia as the main threat to American values reached a new level of intensity, presenting the Kremlin as winning the information war and infiltrating the country. The political divide that pushed the mainstream media toward embracing the new narrative of Trump-Russia "collusion" was largely internal. The divide has roots in the United States' crisis of identity and political polarization. The media that criticized Trump were largely supportive of Hillary Clinton and her vision of a liberal world order with America as its guarantor. However, the 2016 elections also revealed various constituencies within and outside of the Republican Party critical of the mainstream liberal perspective. The US presidential elections exacerbated the already existing divide over the country's role in the world, with Russia serving as a tool for accentuating two principally different visions—globalist and nationalist. This stage of the media's Russophobia was especially dangerous because it involved large segments of the population becoming dependent on the Russia-threat image for America's own psychological confidence. If the United States and Russia fail to foster a constructive dialogue, one can expect the US media to continue the ideological and highly negative coverage of Russia.

Future Clashes of Values

As the world is transitioning toward a new international system, the struggle for power intensifies, and it involves values. The three factors identified in the book—historically developed cultural differences, interstate tensions, and internal political divisions—are likely to complicate future international relations, making cooperation more difficult and conflicts more intense. In a world of growing interstate disagreements, the involvement of larger societies mobilized by media in support of national values promises to play a destabilizing role. Societies that are armed with exclusive and nationalist visions and are prepared to scapegoat others tend to push governments toward confrontation and away from negotiations and the search for compromise. Those responsible for producing and spreading nationally exclusive discourses ought to remember the lessons of the media's role in mobilizing mass nationalist sentiments, and these sentiments' subsequent pressures for militarism.[15]

In the polarized world of international competition and rivalry, value competition is not likely to take the form of a new cold war. Despite all the disagreements, there is no sharp ideological divide between Russia and other non-Western nations on the one hand, and the United States and Europe on the other—they agree on some issues, while sharply disagreeing on others. Their values are different, but not so fundamentally conflicting that would not allow for their coexistence. A much greater ideological division in the world is between secularism and radical Islamism,[16] and that division affects both Russia and the West, alongside Muslim countries. There are other ideological divides *within*, rather than between, nations such as those between liberals and conservatives. None of the existing powers has a Cold War mindset or thinks of others in the familiar ideological terms—either we destroy them or they will destroy us. Nor are the two parties in a comparable military position that may be classified as power poles. Rather, we have multiple actors that may enter into flexible coalitions in order to protect their parochial values and interests.

The lack of ideological conflict notwithstanding, the intense rivalry for power and rules means a greater likelihood of culture wars in world politics. The room for soft power or positive image projection is likely to shrink. When Joseph Nye first introduced the concept of soft power, he meant to highlight the growing prominence of American values and the importance of sharing them for economic and political success in the increasingly global world.[17] Soft power is the ability to influence others by example, thereby encouraging cooperation, not competition, among states. At the time, US power was at its historic peak, and other nations were flocking to win its political and economic support. However, in this new age of transition, competition and confrontation are at least as important as cooperation—not least in the area of values, media, and ideas. Many non-Western nations, such as Russia, China, and Iran, feel threatened by the US strategy of regime change in the Middle East, to which they respond by promoting their own values.

The world is experiencing new processes of cultural reformulations and ethnic nationalism. Instead of relying on the protection and welfare of the US hegemony, nations increasingly seek refuge in developing national and regional arrangements. It would be a mistake to think of Russia's turn to patriotism and conservative values as the Kremlin's exclusive invention. Many others states are looking to build protective "software" in order to rally masses behind their new national identity projects. These projects are largely inward looking, and soft power is a misleading concept for describing their nature. Besides, as chapter 3 documents, the United States itself long moved away from its initial preoccupation with soft power.

Conflicts of values in international relations are therefore likely to continue and intensify. When there are few internationally recognized rules, there is a greater incentive to compete, rather than rely on the power of example. Great powers will continue to seek consolidation of their perceived spheres of influence, even as they try to avoid directly engaging each other. Until a new balance of military power and new rules are established, soft-power projects will have a limited appeal. Based on this book's findings, one can expect value clashes in international relations to take place when state interests over the future world order conflict, and value compromises to occur when state interests coincide or overlap. Exceptions may include cases with gross violation of human rights, such as those that took place in Rwanda in 1992, which policymakers cannot ignore—even if they want to—for domestic political reasons. Other exceptions would include cases of intense ideological rivalry, which are—for the described reasons—all but missing in the contemporary world.

This book found evidence of the value clash between the United States and Russia as resulting from their increasingly different political interests and agendas regarding the international system. Additional evidence of the theory could include examples of Washington's intense value-based criticisms directed at other revisionist powers, and muted criticism toward those that do not seek to undermine the US role in the system. The former can be found in relationships between the United States and China or Iran. Both China and Iran have challenged US dominance in Asia and the Middle East, respectively, and both have come under strong criticisms from Washington on human rights grounds. Indeed, even nations with similar values may demonstrate a considerable potential for conflict when their preferences diverge. Suffice it to recall the intense negative rhetoric in American political and media circles over France's and Germany's decision not to support the US military invasion of Iraq in March 2003. In attempting to isolate major European countries, Secretary of Defense Donald Rumsfeld distinguished "New Europe" from "Old Europe" distinction, whereas some Americans went as far as to return their medals from World War II to the French embassy and to propose renaming French fries as "freedom fries."[18]

On the other hand, there are multiple examples of value compromises when state interests do not conflict. For example, the United States was often critical of the human rights record of its Middle Eastern allies and partners, yet their relationships never escalated to the level of the emotional value clashes with Russia. Even Turkey's bad human rights record did not lead to a break in political relations with Istanbul—in part because, in spite of various differences between the two, the United States and Turkey have been guided by agreement on some principal issues in the region, including methods of stabilizing Syria and Iraq. While visiting Saudi Arabia in May 2017, Donald Trump proposed establishing an "Arab NATO" in order to jointly fight terrorism and contain Iran.[19] Another example is US-Russia relations under George W. Bush. Despite Russia's departure from Western values, Bush continued to view Putin as a partner and a potential ally in the war on terror in part because the Kremlin did not principally challenge Washington's perspective on the world order until later. Similar observations can be made with respect to relations between Obama and Medvedev's during 2008–2011.

Overall, future global clashes of values are likely to occur in those places where states lack internal confidence and where their preferences over the international system conflict. As the world moves toward a multipolar system, value standards are likely to change. Instead of one hegemonic power defining and shaping such standards, several powers will be actively promoting their preferred models of domestic governance and ruling. In the words of a prominent scholar of international relations, the contemporary challenge is "to establish a concept of order *within* the various regions, and to relate these regional orders to one another."[20] As a result, the world is likely to become even more complex and messy than it already is.

NOTES

Preface

1. *Zasedaniye Mezhdunarodnogo diskussionnogo kluba Valdai*, Sochi, October 22, 2015 (all translations not otherwise attributed are mine), http://kremlin.ru/events/president/news/50548.

Chapter 1

1. For definitions and research on values, beliefs, and principles in international politics, see especially C. Reus-Smit, *The Moral Purpose of the State: Culture, Social Identity, and Institutional Rationality in International Relations* (Princeton, NJ: Princeton University Press, 1999); Sonia Lucarelli and Ian Manners, eds., *Values and Principles in European Union Foreign Policy* (New York: Routledge, 2006); Richard Ned Lebow, *National Identities and International Relations* (Cambridge: Cambridge University Press, 2016).
2. Reus-Smit, *Moral Purpose*, 5.
3. Karl Mannheim, *Ideology and Utopia: An Introduction to the Sociology of Knowledge* (Eastford, CT: Martino Fine Books, [1936], 2015), 190.
4. James Goldgeier and Michael McFaul, *Power and Purpose: U.S. Policy toward Russia after the Cold War* (Washington, DC: Brookings Institution Press, 2003); Angela Stent, *Limits of Partnership: US-Russian Relations in the Twenty-First Century* (Princeton, NJ: Princeton University Press, 2014). For a more historically sensitive approach, see Charles Ziegler, "Russian-American Relations: From Tsarism to Putin," *International Politics* 51, no. 6 (2014): 671–92.
5. Walter Russell Mead, *Special Providence: American Foreign Policy and How It Changed the World* (London: Routledge, 2002); Anatol Lieven, *America Right or Wrong: Anatomy of American Nationalism* (New York: Oxford University Press, 2004); David P. Forsythe and Patrice C. McMahon, *American*

Exceptionalism Reconsidered: U.S. Foreign Policy, Human Rights, and World Order (London: Routledge, 2017); Ted Hopf, *Social Construction of International Politics: Identities and Foreign Policies, Moscow, 1955 and 1999* (Ithaca, NY: Cornell University Press, 2002); Robert Legvold, ed., *Russian Foreign Policy in the Twenty-First Century and the Shadow of the Past* (New York: Columbia University Press, 2007); Anne L. Clunan, *The Social Construction of Russia's Resurgence: Aspirations, Identity, and Security Interests* (Baltimore: Johns Hopkins University Press, 2009); Andrei P. Tsygankov, *Russia's Foreign Policy: Change and Continuity in National Identity*, 4th ed. (Lanham, MD: Rowman & Littlefield, 2016); Roger E. Kanet, ed., *The Russian Challenge to the European Security Environment* (New York: Palgrave, 2017).

6. Stephen F. Cohen, *The Failed Crusade: America and the Tragedy of Post-Communist Russia* (New York: Norton, 2001); David Foglesong, *The American Mission and the "Evil Empire": The Crusade for a "Free Russia" since 1881* (Cambridge: Cambridge University Press, 2007); E. Ya. Batalov, V. Yu. Zhuravleva, and K. V. Khozinskaya, *Rychashchiy medved' na 'dikov Vostoke' (Obrazu sovremennoi Rossiyi v rabotakh sovremennykh amerikanskikh avtorov)* (Moscow: Rosspen, 2009); Veronika Krasheninnikova, *Rossiya-America: kholodnaya voina kul'tur* (Moscow: Yevropa, 2013).

7. Henry Hale, *Patronal Politics: Eurasian Regime Dynamics in Comparative Perspective* (Cambridge: Cambridge University Press, 2014); Andrei P. Tsygankov, *The Strong State in Russia: Development and Crisis* (Oxford: Oxford University Press, 2015).

8. Bronfenbrenner, "Mirror Image"; Symon Dalby, "Geopolitical Discourse: The Soviet Union as Other," *Alternatives: Global, Local, Political* 13 (October 1988): 415–42.

9. Foglesong, *American Mission*.

10. Robert Legvold, *Return to Cold War* (Cambridge: Polity Press, 2016); Stephen Cohen, *Why Cold War Again? How America Lost Post-Soviet Russia* (London: I.B. Tauris, 2017).

11. Andrei Kozyrev, "Rossiya v novom mire," *Mezhdunarodnaya zhizn'* 3–4 (1992): 93.

12. Vladimir Putin, "Rossiya na rubezhe tysyacheletiy," *Nezavisimaya gazeta*, December 31, 1999.

13. Andrei P. Tsygankov, *Russophobia: Anti-Russian Lobby and American Foreign Policy* (London: Palgrave, 2009).

14. Gary Hart, "Don't Lose Russia," *National Interest*, March–April 2007).

15. Stephen Cohen, "New Cold War between United States and Russia," *The Charlie Rose Show*, PBS, June 28, 2006, excerpt at Johnson's Russia List, July 2, 2006, No. 149.

16. Andrei P. Tsygankov, "The Dark Double: The American Media Perception of Russia as a Neo-Soviet Autocracy, 2008–2014," *Politics* 37, no. 1 (June 2016): 19–35; Nicholas Ross Smith, "The Re-emergence of a 'Mirror Image' in West-Russia Relations?," *International Politics* 55 (2018): 575–94.
17. The expression is that of George W. Bush (George W. Bush, "Securing Freedom's Triumph," *New York Times*, September 11, 2002).
18. Donald Kagan, Gary James Schmitt, and Thomas Donnelly, *Rebuilding America's Defenses: Strategy, Forces and Resources for a New Century* (Washington, DC: Project for the New American Century, September 2000).
19. Ellen Barry, "New U.S. Envoy Steps into Glare of a Russia Eager to Find Fault," *New York Times*, January 23, 2012.
20. For instance, in February 2016, the BBC released the documentary *Putin's Secret Riches*, in which a US Treasury official stated that Putin is corrupt because he enriches his friends. The White House spokesperson, John Ernest, backed the statement (Press Briefing by Press Secretary Josh Earnest, February 4, 2016, https://www.whitehouse.gov/the-press-office/2016/02/05/press-briefing-press-secretary-josh-earnest-242016).
21. Press Conference with President Obama and Prime Minister Rutte of the Netherlands, March 25, 2014, https://www.whitehouse.gov/the-press-office/2014/03/25/press-conference-president-obama-and-prime-minister-rutte-netherlands.
22. Michael McFaul, "Confronting Putin's Russia," *New York Times*, March 24, 2014.
23. In his inaugural address, Trump drew a contrast between "American carnage" and American greatness, promising to transfer power from Washington to the American people and be guided by the America-first principle (Donald Trump, Inaugural Address, White House, January 20, 2017, https://www.whitehouse.gov/inaugural-address).
24. Robert David English, "Russia, Trump, and a New Détente," *Foreign Affairs*, March 10, 2017, https://www.foreignaffairs.com/articles/russian-federation/2017-03-10/russia-trump-and-new-d-tente?cid=int-lea&pgtype=hpg.
25. Background to "Assessing Russian Activities and Intentions in Recent US Elections," January 6, 2017, https://www.dni.gov/files/documents/ICA_2017_01.pdf.
26. Susan B. Glasser, "Our Putin," *New York Times*, February 18, 2017.
27. Paul Krugman, "Donald Trump, the Siberian Candidate," *New York Times*, July 22, 2016.
28. Stephen Cohen, "Media Contempt for Facts Grows along with the Dangers of War with Russia," *The Nation*, June 28, 2017; Stephen Cohen, "Russiagate or Intelgate?," *The Nation*, February 7, 2018; Glenn Greenwald, "Yet Another Major Russia Story Falls Apart. Is Skepticism Permissible Yet?," *The Intercept*, September 28, 2017; Robert Parry, "Protecting the Shaky Russia-Gate Narrative," *Consortium News*, December 15, 2017; Pat Buchanan, "Time to Get

Over the Russophobia," *American Conservative*, March 8, 2018; Jack F. Matlock Jr., "Contacts with Russian Embassy," March 4, 2017, http://jackmatlock.com/2017/03/contacts-with-russian-embassy/.

29. See, for example, an attack on Stephen Cohen, in which he is called "the Kremlin's No. 1 American apologist" (Cathy Young, "Putin's Pal," *Slate*, July 24, 2014). In a different commentary, *New York Magazine* attributed to Glenn Greenwald a "bunker mentality," a "built-in distrust of national-security apparatuses," and a lack of patriotism (Simon van Zuylen-Wood, "Does Glenn Greenwald Know More Than Robert Mueller?," *New York Magazine*, January 21, 2018).

30. Masha Gessen, a prominent Putin critic who nevertheless challenged the narrative of Trump-Kremlin "collusion," was widely called a "Putin shill," someone whom Putin either bought or forced to speak this way ("Journalists Argue Russian Interference Has Been Exaggerated," *NPR*, March 1, 2018, https://www.npr.org/2018/03/01/589802123/journalists-argue-russian-interference-has-been-exaggerated?sc=tw).

31. Culture, in the words of Arnold Toynbee, "is a movement and not a condition, a voyage and not a harbour" (Arnold Toynbee, *Civilization on Trial* [Oxford: Oxford University Press, 1948], 55).

32. Jan Zielonka, "Empire and Modern Geopolitical System," *Geopolitics* 17 (2012): 502–27.

33. Marcel H. Van Herpen, *Putin's Propaganda Machine: Soft Power and Russian Foreign Policy* (Boulder, CO: Rowman & Littlefield, 2015).

34. Peter Pomerantsev, *Nothing Is True and Everything Is Possible* (New York: Public Affairs, 2014).

35. Yuval Weber and Andrew Krickovic, "Why a Cold War with Russia Is Inevitable," September 30, 2015, *Order from Chaos*, http://www.brookings.edu/blogs/order-from-chaos/posts/2015/09/30-new-cold-war-with-russia-krickovic-weber.

36. Gallup polls, http://www.gallup.com/poll/1642/russia.aspx.

37. Eduard Ponarin, "Russia's Elite: What They Think of the United States and Why," PONARS Eurasia Policy Memo No. 273, August 2013.

38. Lisa Gaufman, *Security Threats and Public Perceptions: Digital Russia and the Ukraine Crisis* (London: Palgrave, 2017).

39. David Campbell, *Writing Security: United States Foreign Policy and the Politics of Identity* (Minneapolis: University of Minnesota Press, 1992); Martha L. Cottam, *Images and Intervention: U.S. Policies in Latin America* (Pittsburgh: University of Pittsburgh Press, 1994); Mark Lynch, *State Interests and Public Spheres* (New York: Columbia University Press, 1999); O. Turner, "'Threatening' China and US Security: The International Politics of Identity," *Review of International Studies* 39 (2013): 903–24; Ronald R. Krebs, "How Dominant Narratives Rise and Fall: Military Conflict, Politics, and the Cold War Consensus," *International Organization* 69, no. 4 (2015): 809–45.

40. Kari Hafez, *The Myth of Media Globalization* (Cambridge: Polity Press, 2007).

41. Johan M. G. Van der Dennen, "Ethnocentrism and In-Group/Out-Group Differentiation: A Review and Interpretation of the Literature," in *The Sociobiology of Ethnocentrism: Evolutionary Dimensions of Xenophobia, Discrimination, Racism and Nationalism*, edited by Vernon Reynolds, Vincent S. E. Falgar, and Ian Vine (London: Croom Helm, 1987), 1.
42. Alister Miskimmon, Ben O'Loughlin, and Laura Roselle, *Strategic Narratives: Communication Power and the New World Order* (London: Routledge, 2013), 2. For earlier work on media and narratives, see Arthur Asa Berger, *Narratives in Popular Culture, Media, and Everyday Life* (London: Sage, 1997). More recently, see Krebs, "How Dominant Narratives Rise."
43. Edward W. Said, *Orientalism* (New York: Vintage Books, 1978); Edward W. Said, *Covering Islam: How the Media and the Experts Determine How We See the Rest of the World*, rev. ed. (New York: Vintage, 1997).
44. R. M. Entman, *Projections of Power: Framing News, Public Opinion, and U.S. Foreign Policy* (Chicago: University of Chicago Press, 2009), 147. For sources on media framing, see the recent overview by Michael A. Cacciatore and Dietram A. Scheufele, "The End of Framing as We Know It . . . and the Future of Media Effects," *Mass Communication and Society* 19, no. 1 (2016): 7–23.
45. Richard Herrmann, *Perceptions and Behavior in Soviet Foreign Policy* (Pittsburgh: University of Pittsburgh Press, 1985); Cottam, *Images and Intervention*.
46. John Mearsheimer, *Why Leaders Lie: The Truth about Lying in International Politics* (New York: Oxford University Press, 2011). For some other works on media coverage during international crises, see Greg Simons, *Mass Media and Modern Warfare: Reporting on the Russian War on Terrorism* (London: Routledge, 2010); Oliver Boyd-Barrett, *Western Mainstream Media and the Ukraine Crisis: A Study in Conflict Propaganda* (London: Routledge, 2016).
47. Edward S. Herman and Noam Chomsky, *Manufacturing Consent* (New York: Pantheon, 1988); Boyd-Barrett, *Western Mainstream Media*.
48. Andrei P. Tsygankov, *Russia and the West from Alexander to Putin* (Cambridge: Cambridge University Press, 2012). For various analyses of Russian values, see Nikolai Rabotyazhev, "Rossiyskaya natsional'naya identichnost' v zerkale sovremennogo otechesetvennogo konservaizma," *Politiya* 70, no. 3 (2013): 62–84; Elena Chebankova, "Contemporary Russian Liberalism," *Post-Soviet Affairs* 30, no. 5 (2014): 341–69; Elena Chebankova, "Contemporary Russian Conservatism," *Post-Soviet Affairs* 32, no. 1 (2016): 28–54.
49. Frank Lambert, *The Founding Fathers and the Place of Religion in America* (Princeton, NJ: Princeton University Press, 2003). For other recent work on American values of religious freedom and individualism, see, for example, Kenneth D. Wald and Allison Calhoun-Brown, *Religion and Politics in the United States* (Boulder, CO: Rowman & Littlefield, 2014).
50. For analyses of Russian media, see Sarah Oates, "The Neo-Soviet Model of the Media," *Europe-Asia Studies* 59, no. 8 (2007): 1279–97; Ellen Mickiewicz,

Television, Power, and the Public in Russia (New York: Cambridge University Press, 2009); Simons, *Mass Media*; Nikolay Petrov, Maria Lipman, and Henry E. Hale, "Three Dilemmas of Hybrid Regime Governance: Russia from Putin to Putin," *Post-Soviet Affairs* (2013): 1–26;; Vera Tolz and Steven Hutchins, *Nation, Ethnicity, and Race on Russian Television: Mediating Post-Soviet Differences* (London: Routledge, 2015); Greg Simons, "Media and Public Diplomacy," in *The Routledge Handbook of Russian Foreign Policy*, edited by Andrei P. Tsygankov (London: Routledge, 2018); Rutger von Seth, "All Quiet on the Eastern Front? Media Images of the West and Russian Foreign Political Identity," *Europe-Asia Studies* 70 (2018): 421–40.

Chapter 2

1. For important research on beliefs and emotions in international politics, see especially Richard Ned Lebow, *The Tragic Vision of Politics: Ethics, Interests and Orders* (Cambridge: Cambridge University Press, 2003); Jonathan Mercer, "Emotional Beliefs," *International Organization* 64 (2010): 1–34; Renee Jeffery, *Reason and Emotion in International Ethics* (Cambridge: Cambridge University Press, 2014); Todd H. Hall, *Emotional Diplomacy: Official Emotion on the International Stage* (Ithaca, NY: Cornell University Press, 2015); Jörg Friedrichs, "An Intercultural Theory of International Relations: How Self-Worth Underlies Politics among Nations," *International Theory* 8, no. 1 (March 2016): 63–96; Robin Markwica, *Emotional Choices: How the Logic of Affect Shapes Coercive Diplomacy* (New York: Oxford University Press, 2018).
2. The literature in psychology associated with social identity theory supports the findings about ethnocentrism. In particular, scholars argue that out-group discrimination and hostility are reinforced by social structural conditions. For a helpful review, see Esra Cuhadar and Bruce Dayton, "The Social Psychology of Identity and Inter-group Conflict," *International Studies Review* 12 (2011): 273–93.
3. Rose McDermott, Nicole Wernimont, and Cheryl Koopman, "Applying Psychology to International Studies: Challenges and Opportunities in Examining Traumatic Stress," *International Studies Review* 12 (2011): 119–35.
4. Naeem Inayatullah and David Blaney, *International Relations and the Problem of Difference* (London: Routledge, 2004).
5. Scholars have analyzed these processes by building on sociological notion of anomie and psychological theories of identity crisis (Brent J. Steele, *Ontological Security in International Relations* [London: Routledge, 2008]; Ayse Zarakol, *After Defeat: How the East Learned to Live with the West* [Cambridge: Cambridge University Press, 2010]; Stefano Guzzini, ed., *The Return of Geopolitics in Europe?*

Social Mechanisms and Foreign Policy Identity Crises [Cambridge: Cambridge University Press, 2012]).
6. Manuel Castells, "Communication, Power and Counter-power in the Network Society," *International Journal of Communication* 1 (2007): 242.
7. Grigori Yavlinski, "Druzhba na vremya ili soyuz navsegda?," *Obschaya gazeta*, January 24, 2002; Valeri Fedorov, "Vperyed, k ideologiyi?," *Nezavisimaya gazeta*, February 18, 2002.
8. Sergey Ptichkin and Aleksey Chichkin, "From Where Russia Is Clearly Visible," *Rossiyskaya Gazeta*, January 22, 2002 (as translated by *CDI Russia Weekly*, No. 190, January 25, 2002).
9. Katrina Vanden Heuvel and Stephen F. Cohen, "Endangering US Security," *The Nation*, April 15, 2002.
10. For details of the Russian discourse, see Andrei P. Tsygankov, "The Final Triumph of the Pax Americana," *Communist and Post-Communist Studies* 34 (1999): 133–56.
11. Valentina Feklyunina, "Constructing Russophobia," in *Russia's Identity in International Relations: Images, Perceptions, Misperceptions*, edited by Ray Taras (London: Routledge, 2012), 93.
12. Tsygankov, *Russophobia*, 38–45.
13. W. Lance Bennett, "Toward a Theory of Press-State Relations in the United State," *Journal of Communication* 40 (1990): 103–23; W. Lance Bennett, "A Semi-independent Press: Government Control and Journalistic Autonomy in the Political Construction of News," *Political Communication* 20 (2003): 381–414.
14. "Rupert Murdoch," *Right Web Profile* (Silver City, NM, March 21, 2007) http://rightweb.irc-online.org.
15. Ibid.
16. Joseph Nye, *Soft Power: The Means to Success in World Politics* (New York: Public Affairs, 2004).
17. J. M. Godzimirski, "What Makes Dialogue and Diplomacy Work or Not? Russia-Georgia and Russia-Ukraine," in *Dialogue and Conflict Resolution: Potential and Limits*, edited by Pernille Rieker and Henrik Thune (Burlington, VT: Ashgate, 2015); Ivan Katchanovski, "The Far Right in Ukraine during the 'Euromaidan' and the War in Donbas," September 2, 2016, available at SSRN: https://ssrn.com/abstract=2832203 or http://dx.doi.org/10.2139/ssrn.2832203.
18. Cited in Eufrosina Dvoichenko-Markov, "Jefferson and the Russian Decembrists," *American Slavic and East European Review* 9, no. 3 (October 1950): 165.
19. On American perception of abolition of serfdom in Russia, see Ivan Kurilla, "Abolition of Serfdom in Russia and American Newspaper and Journal Opinion," in *New Perspectives on Russian-American Relations*, edited by William Benton Whisenhunt and Norman E. Saul (London: Routledge, 2016).

20. "The National Character Is Far from Being Savage," *New-York Magazine*, May 5, 1792 as reproduced in *The American Image of Russia: 1775–1917*, edited by Eugene Anschel (New York: Ungar, 1975), 36. For analysis of early U.S.-Russia contacts, see Norman Saul, *Distant Friends: The United States and Russia, 1763–1867* (Lawrence: University Press of Kansas, 1991).
21. Sean Guillory, "A Genealogy of American Russophobia," *In Russia*, April 17, 2017. For a historical analysis of European Russophobia, see Gay Mettan, *Creating Russophobia: From the Great Religious Schism to Anti-Putin Hysteria* (New York: Clarity Press, 2017).
22. See especially Lieven, *America Right or Wrong* and Foglesong, *American Mission*.
23. Jerald A. Combs, *The History of American Foreign Policy* (New York: McGraw-Hill, 1997), 161–62.
24. George Kennan was a distant cousin of the diplomat George F. Kennan, who was the US ambassador the USSR and author of containment doctrine. On the role of the former Kennan, see Jane E. Good, "America and the Russian Revolutionary Movement, 1888–1905," *Russian Review* 41, no. 3 (1982): 273–87 and Foglesong, *American Mission*, 7–33.
25. Foglesong, *American Mission*, 43–44.
26. Ibid., 109.
27. Cohen, *Failed Crusade*.
28. Various researchers found the US media to be dependent on negative stereotypes and narratives of otherness. For examples, see Ivan Katchanovski and Alicen R. Morley, "The Politics of U.S. Television Coverage of Post-Communist Countries," *Problems of Post-Communism* 59, no. 1 (2012): 15–30; O. Bayulgen and E. Arbatli, "Cold War Redux in US–Russia Relations? The Effects of US Media Framing and Public Opinion of the 2008 Russia-Georgia War," *Communist and Post-Communist Studies* 46 (2013): 513–27.
29. Tsygankov, "The Dark Double"; Smith, "Re-emergence."
30. Jeffrey M. Jones, "Confidence in U.S. Institutions Still below Historical Norms," *Gallup*, June 15, 2015, http://www.gallup.com/poll/183593/confidence-institutions-below-historical-norms.aspx.
31. Anne Applebaum, "War in Europe Is Not a Hysterical Idea," *Washington Post*, August 29, 2014; Timothy Snyder, "Putin's New Nostalgia," *New York Review of Books*, November 10, 2014.
32. See their responses to John Mearsheimer in *Foreign Affairs*, November–December 2014.
33. Patrick Lawrence, "The Perils of Russophobia," *The Nation*, December 29, 2016.
34. For example, see Timothy Snyder, "We Lost a War: Russia's Interference in Our Election Was Much More Than Simple Mischief-Making," *New York Daily News*, March 19, 2017.
35. For analyses of Freedom House's inherent neoconservative bias, see Diego Giannone, "Political and Ideological Aspects in the Measurement

of Democracy: The Freedom House Case," *Democratization* 17, no. 1 (2010): 68–97 and Andrei P. Tsygankov and David Parker, "The Securitization of Democracy: Freedom House Ratings of Russia," *European Security* 24 (2015): 77–100.
36. Kenneth A. Osgood, "Hearts and Minds: The Unconventional Cold War," *Journal of Cold War Studies* 4, no. 2 (2002): 85–107.
37. William Pfaff, "Redefining World Power," *Foreign Affairs* 70, no. 1 (1991): 48.
38. Examples may include Paula J. Dobriansky, "U.S. Needs a Strong Moral Narrative to Combat Putin," *Washington Post*, May 24, 2014; Ilan Berman, "Wanted: A Real War of Ideas with Russia," *National Interest*, July 3, 2014; Daniel Kennedy, "Who's Afraid of Russia Today? Is RT (Formerly Russia Today) Really as Dangerous or as Effective as Its Critics Claim?," *www.opendemocracy.net*, December 5, 2014; Nicole Gaouette, "Sanctions-Strapped Russia Outguns the U.S. in Information War: Moscow Drowns Out Voice of America, and Facts Are a Casualty," *Bloomberg*, April 2, 2015; Ed Royce, "Countering Putin's Information Weapons of War," *Wall Street Journal*, April 15, 2015; Anne Applebaum and Edward Lucas, "Putin's News Network of Lies Is Just the Start," *Newsweek.com*, August 11, 2015; David J. Kramer, "The West Should Take on the Putin P.R. Machine," *Washington Post*, October 25, 2015.
39. Country Reports on Human Rights Practices—2007, US Department of State, March 11, 2008, http://www.state.gov/g/drl/rls/hrrpt/2007/100581.htm.
40. Ruth Deyermond, "Reset or Disconnected? Russian Media and Internet Freedom as a Site of Contestation in US-Russia Relations and US Domestic Politics," paper presented at the International Studies Association Annual Meeting, April 1–4, 2012, San Diego.
41. "Hillary Clinton Declares International Information War," *Russia Today*, March 2, 2011, https://www.rt.com/news/information-war-media-us/.
42. James Carden, "Uncle Sam Got a Shiny New Propaganda Bullhorn for Christmas: A New Partnership Is Turning Radio Free Europe into an Anti-Russia Propaganda Machine," *The Nation*, January 5, 2016.
43. "It's Worse Than You Thought: The 'Kremlin Troll Army' Exposed," *Sputnik*, March 28, 2015.
44. Royce, "Countering Putin's Information Weapons.".
45. Chapter 5 elaborates on US perception of Russia since the election of Trump as president.

Chapter 3

1. Zbigniew Brzezinski, *The Grand Failure: The Birth and Death of Communism in the Twentieth Century* (New York: Collier Books, 1989).
2. Francis Fukuyama, "The End of History?," *National Interest* 16 (Summer 1989): 4.

3. Marc C. Plattner, "Democracy Outwits the Pessimists," *Wall Street Journal*, October 12, 1988.
4. Charles Krauthammer, "The Unipolar Moment," *Foreign Affairs* 70, no. 1 (1991): 23–33.
5. Foglesong, *American Mission*, 204.
6. Michal Specter, "The World—This Russian Democrat May Bury His Cause," *New York Times*, May 5, 1996.
7. Cohen, *Failed Crusade*, 13.
8. Zbigniew Brzezinski, national security advisor to President Jimmy Carter, was among the first to question the wisdom of pursuing what he called a policy of idealistic optimism (Zbigniew Brzezinski, "Premature Partnership," *Foreign Affairs* 73, no. 2 (1994): 67 – 82.
9. Foglesong, *American Mission*, 209.
10. Ibid., 215.
11. William Safire, "Strategic Dilemma," *New York Times*, December 1, 1994; Zbigniew Brzezinski, "A Geostrategy for Eurasia," *Foreign Affairs* 76, no. 5 (1997): 50–64.
12. Goldgeier and McFaul, *Power and Purpose*, 141.
13. Mike Bowker, "Western Views of the Chechen Conflict," in *Chechnya: From Past to Future*, edited by Richard Sakwa (London: Anthem Press, 2006).
14. Richard Pipes, "Is Russia Still an Enemy?" *Foreign Affairs* 76, no. 5 (1997): 67.
15. Safire, "Strategic Dilemma."
16. "Moscow's Mistrust," *Washington Post*, editorial, July 1, 2010.
17. Other scholars have found the analysis of editorials methodologically appropriate for capturing the broader ideological narrative and "media sociocultural identities" (F. Izadi and H. Saqhave-Biria, "A Discourse Analysis of Elite American Newspaper Editorials," *Journal of Communication Inquiry* 31, no. 2, [2007]: 140–65; Elisabeth Le, *Editorials and the Power of Media: Interweaving of Socio-cultural Identities* [Amsterdam: John Benjamins, 2010]). In particular, scholars have studied editorials for the effectiveness of their organizing frames, the degree of synchronization between selection in the news and editorials, and advocacy during wartime (K. C. Smith and M. Wakefield, "Textual Analysis of Tobacco Editorials," *American Journal of Health Promotion* 19, no. 5 [2005]: 361–68; M. Ryan, "Framing the War against Terrorism: US Newspaper Editorials and Military Action in Afghanistan," *International Communication Gazette* 66, no. 5 [2004]: 363–82; C. Elders, "Synchronization of Issue Agendas in News and Editorials of the Prestige Press in Germany," *Communications* 24, no. 3 [1999]: 301–28; S. Saff and Y. Ohara, "The Media and the Pursuit of Militarism in Japan," *Critical Discourse Studies* 3, no. 1 [2006]: 81–101).
18. In particular, the *Washington Post* (for the remainder of this chapter abbreviated *WP*) has been the most active, publishing almost twice as many editorials on Russia as the *New York Times* (*NYT*) and the *Wall Street Journal* (*WSJ*). There

were also some differences in the issues each publication chose to cover. Perhaps predictably, the *WSJ* focused on business and property rights more extensively than the other two newspapers. On the other hand, the *WSJ* was the only one of the three that did not comment on gay rights, while both the *NYT* and the *WP* strongly condemned Russia's laws banning the "propaganda of nontraditional sexual relations to minors" as Putin's "war on gays" and a new level of "legitimizing the hatemongering in legislation" ("Mr. Putin's War on Gays," *NYT*, editorial, July 28, 2013; "Russia's War on Gays," *WP*, editorial, August 9, 2013).

19. "Mr. Medvedev's Glasnost," *WP*, editorial, November 14, 2009.
20. "Russia, Disgraced," *WP*, editorial, July 18, 2009; "The Moscow Bombings," *NYT*, editorial, March 31, 2010; "Russia Stirring," *WP*, editorial, December 26, 2011; "Kicking Democracy's Corpse in Russia," *NYT*, editorial, January 30, 2008; "Putin's Memory Hole," *WSJ*, editorial, October 15, 2014; "Wiping Away the Soviet Past," *WP*, editorial, October 16, 2014; "Putin's Disinformation Matrix," *WSJ*, editorial, November 15, 2014; "Russia's Succession," *WP*, editorial, March 2, 2008.
21. "Vladimir Putin's Russia," *NYT*, editorial, February 27, 2008; "Corruptionism," *WP*, editorial, December 26, 2011; "Oil and Capitalism," *WP*, editorial, October 30, 2012; "An Assault on Civil Society," *WP*, editorial, July 21, 2013; "Putin's Disinformation Matrix," *WSJ*.
22. Although some autocracies may develop totalitarian tendencies, most of Russia's autocratic systems were respectful of established social and political boundaries (Nikolai Petro, *The Rebirth of Russian Democracy: An Interpretation of Political Culture* [Cambridge. MA: Harvard University Press, 1995], 33).
23. "Kicking Democracy's Corpse in Russia," *NYT*; "Corruptionism," *WP*; "A Whistleblower in Moscow," *WSJ*, editorial, July 13, 2013; "Moscow's Mistrust," *WP*, editorial, July 1, 2010.
24. "Putin Strengthens His Legacy," *NYT*, editorial, February 13, 2008; "The Winter of Mr. Putin's Discontent," *NYT*, editorial, December 5, 2014; "Mr. Putin Tries to Crush Another Rival," *NYT*, editorial, July 19, 2013; "Improvising in Panic," *WP*, editorial, December 31, 2014.
25. "Mr. Putin's War on Gays," *NYT*, editorial, July 28, 2013.
26. "Russia's Succession," *WP*; "Putin and Navalny," *WSJ*, editorial, April 24, 2014.
27. "President 'Whatever,'" *WSJ*, editorial, March 3, 2008; "Who Ordered Politkovskaya's Murder," *NYT*, editorial, June 11, 2014.
28. A number of observers of US-Russia relations have referred to this as the Putin demonization effect (Stephen F. Cohen, "Stop the Pointless Demonization of Putin," *Reuters*, May 7, 2012; Henry Kissinger, "To Settle the Ukraine Crisis, Start at the End," WP, March 5, 2014).
29. The *Washington Post* expressed a common perception when it backed the British judge Robert Owen's verdict that Putin "probably approved" the assassination of Litvinenko and called for treating its leader as "an outcast," Russia

not "as a normal state" ("Vladimir Putin's Poison Tea," *WP*, editorial, January 24, 2016).
30. "Navalny's Triumph," *WSJ*, editorial, September 10, 2013.
31. "Spring in the Russian Air?," *NYT*, editorial, December 6, 2011; "Mr. Medvedev's Glasnost," *WP*; "Russia's Quiet Repression," *WP*, editorial, August 10, 2014; "A Run on Russia," *WSJ*, editorial, September 18, 2008; "Our Friends the Russians," *WSJ*, editorial, February 13, 2012.
32. "No Monitors, Please—We're Russians," *WP*, editorial, December 4, 2011.
33. Ibid.
34. Denis Volkov, "The Evolution of Anti-Americanism in Russia," Carnegie.ru Commentary, June 22, 2015, http://carnegieendowment.org/2015/06/22/evolution-of-anti-americanism-in-russia/iavh.
35. "Mr. Putin's Counterrevolution," editorial, WP, November 17, 2005.
36. Mark MacKinnon, *The New Cold War: Revolutions, Rigged Elections and Pipeline Politics in the Former Soviet Union* (Toronto: Random House, 2007); Edward Lucas, *The New Cold War: Putin's Russia and the Threat to the West* (London: Palgrave, 2008).
37. Richard Cheney, *Vice President's Remarks at the 2006 Vilnius Conference*, Vilnius, Lithuania: The White House, Office of the Vice President, May 4, 2006, http://georgewbush-whitehouse.archives.gov/news/releases/2006/05/20060504-1.html.
38. Freedom House, *Freedom in the World*, Reports 2005–2013, http://www.freedomhouse.org/report/freedom-world/freedom-world-2005.
39. Arch Puddington, "Back from the Dead," *New York Sun*, October 24, 2006, http://www.freedomhouse.org/article/back-dead.
40. *Russia's Wrong Direction: What the United States Can and Should Do* (New York: Council on Foreign Relations, 2006).
41. John Edwards and Jack Kemp, "We Need to Be Tough with Russia," *International Herald Tribune*, July 12, 2006.
42. McCain as cited in Jackie Calmes, "McCain Sees Something Else in Putin's Eyes," *Washington Wire*, October 16, 2007, http://blogs.wsj.com/washwire/2007/10/16/mccain-sees-something-in-putins-eyes/.
43. Peter Baker and Susan Glasser, *Kremlin Rising: Vladimir Putin's Russia and the End of Revolution* (New York: Simon & Schuster, 2005). See especially chapter 13, "Back in the USSR."
44. Graeme Robertson, *The Politics of Protest in Hybrid Regimes: Managing Dissent in Post-Communist Russia* (Cambridge: Cambridge University Press, 2011); Petrov, Lipman, and Hale, "Three Dilemma.". Medvedev's presidency was not a radical departure from that of Putin, yet it had important differences in priorities. Medvedev's vision included an economy liberated from dependence on energy exports, a more open political system, and stronger ties with Western nations (Dmitry Medvedev, "Go Russia," September 10, 2009, http://en.kremlin.ru/events/president/news/5413).

45. Cohen, "New Cold War"; Hart, "Don't Lose Russia."
46. Vladimir Socor, "Energy Security as a Euro-Atlantic Concern," *Eurasia Daily Monitor*, September 6, 2006; Pavel Baev, "Can Russia Take Its Place in the G8 for Granted?," *Eurasia Daily Monitor*, February 17, 2005.
47. Michael McFaul, "Russia: More Stick, Less Carrot," *Hoover Digest* 1 (2008): 43.
48. Foreign Policy Initiative Letter Asks Obama to Make Human Rights Central to Talks in Russia, *Weekly Standard*, July 1, 2009; D. J. Kramer, "America's Silence Makes Us Complicit in Russia's Crimes," WP, September 20, 2010.
49. For other views on Russia critical of the mainstream perspective, see articles published in the *Anti-War.com*, *Consortium*, *CounterPunch*, and *The Nation*.
50. Slawomir Sierakowski, "Putin's Useful Idiots," NYT, April 28, 2014; Isaac Chotiner, "Meet Vladimir Putin's American Apologist," New Republic, March 2, 2014; Carl Schreck, "Stephen Cohen, Preeminent Scholar, Now Seen as Putin Apologist," *Radio Free Europe / Radio Liberty*, May 6, 2015; Cathy Young, "Stephen Cohen Was Once Considered a Top Russia Historian. Now He Publishes Odd Defenses of Vladimir Putin," *Slate*, July 24, 2014; Mark Hemingway, "It's Not Just Trump Defenders—What about the Pro-Putin Left?," *Weekly Standard*, April 6, 2017; James Kirchick, "Meet the Anti-Semites, Truthers, and Alaska Pol at D.C.'s Pro-Putin Soiree," *Daily Beast*, June 17, 2014.
51. The decision was later reversed in response to a letter of support for Cohen signed by more than 130 members of the association (Hank Reichman, "Russia Scholars Reply to ASEEES 'Detailed Clarification' Regarding Cohen-Tucker Fellowship Controversy," February 9, 2015, https://academeblog.org/2015/02/09/russia-scholars-reply-to-aseees-detailed-clarification-regarding-cohen-tucker-fellowship-controversy/).
52. Bush, "Securing Freedom's Triumph."
53. Jackson Diehl, "Obama's Misguided Wooing of an Uninterested Putin," WP, May 14, 2012; Anders Aslund, "Kick Russia Out of the G-8," *Foreign Policy*, May 15, 2012; Garry Kasparov, "The Myth of a U.S.-Russia Strategic Partnership," WSJ, May 20, 2012; Leon Aron, "Don't Go There: Why President Barack Obama Should Not Visit Russia," *Foreign Policy*, November 20, 2012; Masha Gessen, "The Dictator," NYT, May 21, 2012.
54. David J. Kramer, "President Obama Should Skip Moscow and the Sochi Olympics and It's Not Just Because of Edward Snowden," *American Interest*, July 29, 2013; Carl Gershman, "Former Soviet States Stand Up to Russia. Will the U.S.?," WP, September 27, 2013.
55. Thomas Friedman, "Obama, Snowden and Putin," NYT, August 14, 2013.
56. Bill Keller, "Russia vs. Europe," NYT, December 16, 2013.
57. "Russia passes law banning gay 'propaganda'," https://www.theguardian.com/world/2013/jun/11/russia-law-banning-gay-propaganda.
58. Intellectual influence on the approach included work on strategic communication (R. S. Zaharna, *Battles to Bridges: US Strategic Communication and Public Diplomacy after 9/11* [Basingstoke: Palgrave Macmillan, 2010]; G. Hayden, *The*

Rhetoric of Soft Power: Public Diplomacy in Global Contexts [New York: Lexington Books, 2012]).
59. "Hillary Clinton Declares International Information War," *RT World News*, March 2, 2011, https://www.rt.com/news/information-war-media-us/.
60. Victoria Nuland, "Testimony on Ukraine," Senate Foreign Relations Committee, Washington, DC, October 8, 2015, http://www.state.gov/p/eur/rls/rm/2015/oct/248032.htm.
61. Charles Clover, "Clinton Vows to Thwart New Soviet Union," *Financial Times*, December 7, 2012.
62. Full text of President Obama's 2014 address to the United Nations General Assembly, https://www.washingtonpost.com/politics/full-text-of-president-obamas-2014-address-to-the-united-nations-general-assembly/2014/09/24/88889e46-43f4-11e4-b437-1a7368204804_story.html.
63. Kirill Belyaninov and Gennadi Sysoyev, "Amerika razvedala buduscheye Rossiyi," *Kommersant*, February 2, 2012, http://www.kommersant.ru/doc/1863482.
64. United States International Communications Reform Act of 2014, House of Representatives, July 28, 2014; Chairman Royce. Ranking Member Engel Introduce U.S. International Broadcasting Reform Legislation, April 29, 2014, House Committee on Foreign Relations (cited in Natalya A. Tsvetkova, "Publichnaya diplomatiya SShA," *Mezhdunarodnyye protsessy* 13, no. 3 [2015]: 121–33).
65. Andrei Tsygankov, "Assessing Cultural and Regime-Based Explanations of Russia's Foreign Policy," *Europe-Asia Studies* 64 (2012): 695–713.
66. "Kremlin Hostage Takers," *WSJ*, editorial, December 31, 2014.
67. "Putin's Disinformation Matrix," *WSJ*.
68. Julia Embody, "Beware Ukraine's Rising Right Sector," *National Interest*, August 12, 2015.
69. "Mr. Medvedev's Glasnost," *WP*; "Kremlin Hostage Takers," *WSJ*.
70. "The Run on the Ruble," *WSJ*, editorial, November 3, 2014; "The Ruble's Fall and Mr. Putin's Reckoning," *NYT*, editorial, December 17, 2014.
71. "Putin's Ruble Rout," *WSJ*, editorial, December 16, 2014.
72. Peter Baker, "Obama Team Debates How to Punish Russia," *NYT*, March 12, 2014.
73. McFaul, "Confronting Putin's Russia."
74. "Improvising in Panic," *WP*, editorial, December 31, 2014.
75. Polls demonstrate that Russians tend to prioritize order over democracy. For example, during 2000–2010, over 70% of respondents registered their preference for order, with only around 15% preferring democracy (*RIA Novosti*, April 12, 2010). Until 2014, despite political protest in the late 2011, 52%–60% rated Putin's work favorably (D. Tsoi, "Putin 3.0: kak izmenilos' vospriyatiye prezidenta za 15 let," *RBK*, March 27, 2015, http://top.rbc.ru/politics/27/03/2015/551431a59a7947b6b14097ef). Putin's ratings then improved further

following the annexation of Crimea, yet even the post-Crimean majority in part consisted of pragmatic supporters of Putin. Despite the high level of militarist and anti-Western propaganda in state media, around 60% of Putin's supporters did not want Russia's military intervention in Ukraine and around 40% worried about isolation from the West (A. Titkov, "Tri Rossiyi: iz kogo na samom dele skladyvayetsya 'putinskoye bol'shinstvo," *RBK*, March 30, 2015, http://daily.rbc.ru/opinions/politics/31/03/2015/551a40189a79477151f9b609).

76. "Kremlin Hostage Takers," *WSJ*.
77. "Putin's Disinformation Matrix," *WSJ*.
78. Ibid.
79. Applebaum and Lucas, "Putin's News Network." See also Kramer, "The West Should Take on the Putin P.R. Machine."
80. McFaul, "Confronting Putin's Russia."
81. Dobriansky, "U.S. Needs Strong Moral Narrative"; Berman, "Wanted."
82. "U.S. Comprehensive Strategy toward Russia," *Heritage Foundation*, December 9, 2015.
83. Carden, "Uncle Sam."
84. James Kirchick, "How a U.S. Think Tank Fell for Putin," *Daily Beast*, July 27, 2015.
85. Royce, "Countering Putin's Information Weapons."
86. James Carden, "Neo-McCarthyism and the US Media," *The Nation*, May 20, 2015.
87. Carden, "Uncle Sam."
88. Kennedy, "Who's Afraid."
89. Ibid.
90. "It's Worse Than You Thought: The 'Kremlin Troll Army' Exposed," *Sputnik*, March 28, 2015; Gaouette, "Sanctions-Strapped Russia."
91. Art Swift, "In U.S., Record 68% View Russia as Unfriendly or an Enemy. Putin's favorability dips below 10%," www.gallup.com, March 27, 2014.
92. Ibid.

Chapter 4

1. Van Herpen, *Putin's Propaganda Machine*.
2. Vladimir Shlapentokh, "The Puzzle of Russian Anti-Americanism: From 'Below' or from 'Above,'" *Europe-Asia Studies* 63, no. 5 (2011): 875–89; Petr Pomerantsev, "The Kremlin's Information War," *Journal of Democracy* 25, no. 4 (2015): 40–50.
3. Marcel H. Van Herpen, *Putin's Wars: The Rise of Russia's New Imperialism* (Lanham, MD: Rowman & Littlefield, 2015); Dalia Grybauskaite, "Russia Is

a Threat . . . to All of Europe," *Foreign Policy*, March 24, 2017; Daniel Fried, "Russia's Back-to-the-80s Foreign Policy," *The Atlantic*, August 2, 2017.
4. The Russian economy matched its 1990 in 2005, having lost some fifteen years of development.
5. Andrey Movchan, "How the Sanctions Are Helping Putin," *Politico.com*, March 28, 2017.
6. David White, "State Capacity and Regime Resilience in Putin's Russia," *International Political Science Review* 39, no. 1 (2018): 130–43, http://journals.sagepub.com/doi/abs/10.1177/0192512117694481.
7. See, for example, Aleksandra Samarina, "Ugolovno-administrativnoye stimulirovaniye elit," *Nezavisimaya gazeta*, August 27, 2013.
8. For critical assessments of Russian foreign policy, see Robert Legvold, "Russia's Unreformed Foreign Policy," *Foreign Affairs*, September–October 2001; Roy Allison, *Russia, the West, and Military Intervention* (New York: Oxford University Press, 2013); Dmitry Trenin, *Intregatsiya i identichnost'* (Moscow: Tsentr Karnegi, 2006); Dmitry Trenin, *Rossiya i mir v XXI veke* (Moscow: Aspekt Press, 2015).
9. Scholars investigated how the Soviet disintegration and social anxiety animated various conspiracy theories with respect to the West and its intentions (Stefanie Ortmann and John Heathershaw, "Conspiracy Theories in the Post-Soviet Space," *Russian Review* 71, no. 4 [2012]: 551–64). Some of these conspiracies had old roots, while others were more contextual and created by Russian media to delegitimize policies of the United States (Richard Sakwa, "Conspiracy Narratives as a Mode of Engagement in International Politics: The Case of the 2008 Russo-Georgian War," *Russian Review* 71, no. 4 [2012]: 581–609; Ilya Yablokov, "Conspiracy Theories as a Russian Public Diplomacy Tool: The Case of Russia Today (RT)," *Politics* 35 [2015]: 301–15).
10. Pomerantsev, "The Kremlin's Information War"; N. Maréchal, "Networked Authoritarianism and the Geopolitics of Information: Understanding Russian Internet Policy," *Media and Communication* (2017): 29–41.
11. For a different approach that stresses diversity of cultural and sovereignty discourses and calls for a dialogue among cultures and states, see J. L. Cohen, *Globalization and Sovereignty: Rethinking Legality, Legitimacy, and Constitutionalism* (Cambridge: Cambridge University Press, 2012).
12. Henry Hale, "Eurasian Politics as Hybrid Regimes: The Case of Putin's Russia," *Journal of Eurasian Studies* 1, no. 1 (2010): 33–41; Robertson, *Politics of Protest*; Petrov, Lipman, and Hale, "Three Dilemmas"; J. A. Dunn, "Lottizzazione Russian Style: Russia's Two-Tier Media System," *Europe-Asia Studies* 66, no. 9 (2014): 1425–51; Geir Flikke, "The Sword of Damocles: State Governability in Putin's Third Term," *Problems of Post-Communism* (2017), https://www.tandfonline.com/doi/full/10.1080/10758216.2017.1291308.

13. Monty G. Marshall, *Political Regime Characteristics and Transitions, 1800–2013* (Polity IV, 2014), http://www.systemicpeace.org/polity/polity4x.htm. For other ratings in comparison with Freedom House, see Tsygankov and Parker, "The Securitization of Democracy."
14. For development of this argument, see Tsygankov, *Strong State in Russia*.
15. For comparisons of contemporary Russia to tsarism, see Anna Arutunyan, *The Putin Mystique: Inside Russia's Power Cult* (London: Olive Brunch, 2014); William Zimmerman, *Ruling Russia: Authoritarianism from the Revolution to Putin* (Princeton, NJ: Princeton University Press, 2014); Steven Lee Myers, *The New Russian Tsar: The Rise and Reign of Vladimir Putin* (New York: Vintage, 2016).
16. Boyd-Barrett, *Western Mainstream Media*; Adrian Chen, "The Propaganda about Russian Propaganda," *New Yorker*, December 1, 2016.
17. R. P. Formisano, *Plutocracy in America: How Increasing Inequality Destroys the Middle Class and Exploits the Poor* (Baltimore: John Hopkins University Press, 2015).
18. For criticisms of the autocratic expansion perspective, see Tsygankov, "Assessing Cultural and Regime-Based Explanations"; "Authoritarian at Heart and Expansionist by Habit?," *Europe-Asia Studies* 64, no. 4 (2012): 695–717.
19. Fukuyama, "The End of History." For details of the Russian reaction to Fukuyama, see Tsygankov, *Whose World Order? Russia's Perception of American Ideas after the Cold War* (South Bend, IN: University of Notre Dame Press, 2004), chap. 4.
20. Denis Volkov, "Istoriya rossiyskogo antiamerikanizma," June 8, 2015. http://carnegie.ru/2015/05/27/ru-60220/i9kf.
21. Ibid.
22. For studies of Russian nationalism in the late Soviet and early post-Soviet years, see Yitzhak M. Brudny, *Reinventing Russia: Russian Nationalism and the Soviet State, 1953–1991* (Cambridge. MA: Harvard University Press, 2000); Marlene Laruelle, ed., *Russian Nationalism and the National Reassertion of Russia* (London: Routledge, 2009); Paul Kolstø and Helge Blakkisrud, eds., *The New Russian Nationalism: Imperialism, Ethnicity, and Authoritarianism, 2000–15* (Manchester: Manchester University Pres, 2016); Charles Clover, *Black Wind, White Snow: The Rise of Russia's New Nationalism* (New Haven: Yale University Press, 2016); Richard Arnold, *Russian Nationalism and Ethnic Violence: Symbolic Violence, Lynching, Pogrom and Massacre* (London: Routledge, 2016).
23. Vladimir Sorgin, "Zapadny liberalizm i rossiyskiye reformy," *Svobodnaya mysl'* 1 (1996): 32.
24. Volkov, "Istoriya rossiyskogo antiamerikanizma."
25. William Zimmerman, *The Russian People and Foreign Policy* (Princeton, NJ: Princeton University Press, 2002), 92.
26. Ponarin, "Russia's Elite."

27. Floriana Fossato, "Russia: Moderate Politicians Worried by Internal Consequences Of Kosovo," *Radio Free Europe / Radio Liberty*, April 7, 1999, http://www.russialist.org/archives/3231.html.
28. Lydiya Andrusenko, "Poidet li Rossiya v soyuzniki SShA?," *Nezavisimiya gazeta*, September 21, 2001.
29. Sergei Kortunov, "Rossiysko-amerikanskoye partnerstvo," *Mezhdunarodnaya zhizn'* 2 (2002): 42–69.
30. Milrad Fatullayev, "Voina idet v Rossiyu," *Nezavisimaya gazeta*, November 10, 2001; Dmitri Furman, "Polet dvuglavogo orla," *Obschaya gazeta*, May 30, 2002.
31. *Nezavisimaya gazeta* (for the remainder of this chapter abbreviated *NG*) published 231 editorials and the *New York Times* (*NYT*) 128 editorials during this period. Using the methodology described in chapter 3, note 92 I rated the sides' attitudes toward each other as positive, negative, and neutral by producing and then plotting the score of the media's attitude toward the respective country.
32. "Geopolitika vs. prava cheloveka," *NG*, editorial, September 17, 2008; "Perezagruzka, no bez sfer vliyaniya," *NG*, editorial, March 2, 2009.
33. "Uroki avgusta 2008-go," *NG*, editorial, August 8, 2011.
34. "Tomagavki demokratiyu ne prodvinut," *NG*, editorial, April 7, 2011.
35. "Zhalyashchiy ukol i ekstraditstiya Viktora Buta," *NG*, editorial, November 18, 2010; "Suverennost' I mezhdunarodnoye pravo," *NG*, editorial, December 10, 2010; "Ispytaniye Snoudenom," *NG*, editorial, July 17, 2013.
36. "Chuzhikh ne spasayem," *NG*, editorial, September 17, 2015.
37. "Zachem SShA pugayut staryi svet," *NG*, editorial, April 26, 2010; "Yest' li budushcheye u novoi koalitsiyi," *NG*, editorial, August 13, 2015.
38. "Teni bipolyarnogo mira," *NG*, editorial, December 29, 2014.
39. "Amerikanskaya Stavka v igre protiv Kremlya," *NG*, editorial, June 4, 2014; "Sanktsiyi: nazhim na Kreml' ili prizyv k Maidanu?" *NG*, editorial, December 10, 2014.
40. "Vtoraya popytka Hillari Klinton," *NG*, editorial, March 4, 2015.
41. "Dve nedeli stolknoveniya tsivilizatsiy," *NG*, editorial, September 24, 2012.
42. "Obama ne posledoval primeru Kennedi," *NG*, editorial, November 7, 2013.
43. "Prezident SShA proigryvayet Kongressu," *NG*, editorial, November 21, 2013.
44. "Obame grozit politicheskiy paralich," *NG*, editorial, October 30, 2014.
45. For example, see Alexander Domrin, "SShA: bremya global'nogo liderstva," *Izborsky klub* 1 (2016), http://www.izborsk-club.ru/content/articles/8511/?sphrase_id=23933.
46. "Blesk dollar tuskneyet," *NG*, editorial, July 17, 2009; "Suverennost' I mezhdunarodnoye pravo," *NG*, editorial, December 10, 2010; "God posle Pragi," *NG*, editorial, April 11, 2011; "Za mesto pod solntsem," *NG*, editorial, April 12, 2012.

47. G. Sharafutdinova, "The Pussy Riot Affair and Putin's Démarche from Sovereign Democracy to Sovereign Morality," *Nationalities Papers* 42, no. 4 (2014): 615–21.
48. The US State Department called the punishment "disproportionate" and urged Russian authorities to "ensure that the right to freedom of expression is upheld" (Howard Amos, "Guilty Verdict Puts the Heat on Putin," *Moscow Times*, August 20, 2012).
49. Gaufman, *Security Threats*, 93.
50. Dmitriy Kiselev as cited in Gaufman, *Security Threats*.
51. Ibid.
52. For analyses of the two-tier media system and its relations to the state, see Dunn, "Lottizzazione Russian Style."
53. Aleksander Oslon, ed., *Amerika: vzglyad iz Rossiyi* (Moscow: Institut Fonda "Obschestvennoye mneniye," 2001), 27.
54. Sergey Ptichkin and Aleksey Chichkin, "Otkuda vidna Rossiya," *Rossiyskaya Gazeta*, January 22, 2002.
55. Vladimir Putin, "Poslaniye Federal'nomu Sobraniyu Rossiyskoy Federatsiyi," March 2005, www.kremlin.ru.
56. Vladislav Surkov, "Suvrenitet—eto politicheskiy sinonim konkurentosposobnosti," *Moscow News*, March 3, 2006.
57. For analyses of these developments, see Peter J. S. Duncan, "Russia, the West and the 2007–2008 Electoral Cycle: Did the Kremlin Really Fear a 'Coloured Revolution'?," *Europe-Asia Studies* 65, no. 1 (2013): 1–25.
58. Yekaterina Dobrynina, "Prishli k soglasiyu:," *Rossiyskaya gazeta*, September 6, 2006; Leonid Polyakov, "Suverennaya demokratiya kak professiya i prizvaniye," *Russky zhurnal*, November 24, 2006; Aleksei Chadayev, "Demokratizatsiya nastoyashchego," *Russky zhurnal*, November 29, 2006.
59. James Rodgers, "Russia Acts against 'False' History," *BBC News*, July 24, 2009.
60. The perspective of Baltic and other nations was that Russia was responsible for the occupation. When the Kremlin invited more than fifty foreign leaders to come to Moscow on May 9, 2005, to celebrate victory over fascism in World War II, several Eastern European nations, including Lithuania and Estonia, refused, viewing the end of the war as the beginning of their occupation by the Soviets.
61. Vladimir Putin, "Meeting of the Valdai International Discussion Club," Sochi, October 2013.
62. Vladimir Putin, "Poslaniye Prezidenta Federal'nomu Sobraniyu Rossiyskoy Federatsii," December 13, 2013, http://president.kremlin.ru.
63. Putin, "Samoopredeleniye russkogo naroda," *Nezavisimaya gazeta*, January 23, 2012. Along these lines, the new official nationalities strategy until 2025 signed by Putin in December 2012 reintroduced Russia as a "unique sociocultural civilization entity formed of the multipeople Russian nation" and, under pressures of Muslim constituencies, removed the reference to ethnic Russians as

the core of the state (*Kommersant*, December 19, 2012). For analyses of Russia's civilizational vision, see Tuomas Forsberg and Hanna Smith, "Russian Cultural Statecraft in the Eurasian Space," *Problems of Post-Communism* 63, no. 3 (2016): 129–34; Andrei P. Tsygankov, "Crafting the State-Civilization: Vladimir Putin's Turn to Distinct Values," *Problems of Post-Communism* 63,(no. 3 (2016): 146–58; Fabian Linde, "The Civilizational Turn in Russian Political Discourse: From Pan-Europeanism to Civilizational Distinctiveness," *Russian Review* 74, no. 4 (2016): 604–25; Elena Chebankova, "Russia's Idea of the Multipolar World Order," *Post-Soviet Affairs* 33, no. 3 (2017): 217–34, https://www.tandfonline.com/doi/abs/10.1080/1060586X.2017.1293394; Glenn Diesen, *The Decay of Western Civilization and Resurgence of Russia* (London: Routledge, 2018).

64. Address by President of the Russian Federation, Moscow, Kremlin, March 18, 2014.
65. Vladimir Putin, "Meeting with the Russian Federation Ambassadors," Moscow, Foreign Ministry, July 9, 2012. For Russia's approach to soft power, see Andrei P. Tsygankov, "Russia's Soft Power Strategy," *Current History* 112 (2015): 259–64; Alexander Sergunin and Leonid Karabeshkin, "Understanding Russia's Soft Power Strategy," *Politics* 35, nos. 3–4 (2015): 347–63; Jeanne L. Wilson, "Russia and China Respond to Soft Power: Interpretation and Readaptation of a Western Construct," *Politics* 35, nos. 3–4 (2015): 287–300.
66. Sirke Mäkinen, "In Search of the Status of an Educational Great Power? Analysis of Russia's Educational Diplomacy Discourse," *Problems of Post-Communism* 63, no. 3 (2016): 183–96.
67. Valentina Feklyunina, "Soft Power and Identity: Russia, Ukraine and the 'Russian World(s),'" *European Journal of International Relations* 22, no. 4 (2015): 773–96.
68. Vladimir Putin's Press-Conference, Kremlin.ru, March 4, 2014, http://eng.kremlin.ru/news/6763.
69. Andrei Soldatov, "Reading the World: The Internet and Political Change in Russia," *Foreign Affairs*, April 6, 2016, https://www.foreignaffairs.com/articles/russian-federation/2016-04-06/reading-world.
70. Fareed Zakaria, "Illiberal Democracy," *Foreign Affairs*, November–December 1997.
71. For bottom-up perspectives on Russian media, propaganda, and soft power, see Arkady Ostrovsky, *The Invention of Russia*; Gaufman, *Security Threat*; Vincent Charles Keating and Katarzyna Kaczmarska, "Conservative Soft Power: Liberal Soft Power Bias and the 'Hidden' Attraction of Russia," *Journal of International Relations and Development* (2017), doi: 10.1057/s41268-017-0100-6.
72. Henry E. Hale, "'Trends in Russian Views on Democracy 2008–12: Has There Been a Russian Democratic Awakening?," *Russian Analytical Digest* no. 117, September 19, 2012. For more on Russia's idea of the strong state and its obligations, see Felix Hett and Reinhard Krumm, "The Russian Dream: Justice,

Liberty, and a Strong State," *Russian Analytical Digest* no. 124, March 18, 2013; Tsygankov, *Strong State in Russia*.
73. Hale, "Trends in Russian Views," 5.
74. For example, in December 1999, during his trip to China, Yeltsin rejected the US criticism of Russia's Chechnya intervention by publicly reminding President Bill Clinton that Russia possessed a "full nuclear arsenal" ("Don't Lecture on Chechnya, Yeltsin Reminds Clinton," *Reuters*, December 9, 1999).
75. Interview with *Washington Post*, September 26, 2003, as cited in Baker and Glasser, *Kremlin Rising*, 286.
76. Ol'ga Solovyeva, "Rossiyane soetuyut vlastyam zanyat'sya ekonomikoi," *Nezavisimaya gazeta*, February 16, 2018.
77. Timothy Frye, "Putin's Electoral Result: A Not So Simple Tale," March 21, 2018, https://medium.com/@timothymfrye/putins-electoral-result-a-not-so-simple-tale-7faebaae4627.
78. Samuel Greene and Graeme Robertson, "Putin and the Passions," *Moscow Times*, March 21, 2018.
79. In addition to ordering twenty-three British diplomats to leave Russia, the Kremlin banned activities of the British Council in the country and recalled the license to open a British consulate in St. Petersburg.

Chapter 5

1. Some of the themes in this and next chapter are discussed in Andrei P. Tsygankov, "American Russophobia in the Age of Liberal Decline," *Critique and Humanism* 49, 1, 2018
2. Sharon Burke, "If You Weren't Already Worried about Russia, You Should Be Now," *CNN*, March 25, 2018.
3. Donald Trump, Inaugural Address, January 20, 2017, https://www.whitehouse.gov/inaugural-address.
4. "[Putin] is really very much of a leader. I mean, you can say, oh, isn't that a terrible thing—the man has very strong control over a country. Now, it's a very different system, and I don't happen to like the system. But certainly, in that system, he's been a leader, far more than our president has been a leader" (Ryan Teague Beckwith, "Read Hillary Clinton and Donald Trump's Remarks at a Military Forum," September 07, 2016, http://time.com/4483355/commander-chief-forum-clinton-trump-intrepid/).
5. Krugman, Siberian Candidate."
6. Michael McFaul, "The Real Winner of the House Intelligence Committee Hearing on Russia,", *Washington Post*, March 24, 2017.
7. Snyder, "We Lost a War."

8. Thomas Friedman, "What Trump Is Doing Is Not OK," *New York Times*, February 14, 2017.
9. *Rachel Maddow Show*, March 9, 2017. https://www.youtube.com/watch?v=sInL5kyQklU.
10. Nicholas Kristof, "There's a Smell of Treason in the Air," *New York Times*, March 23, 2017.
11. https://twitter.com/anneapplebaum/status/843523070233133056.
12. Kaitlan Collins and Jeff Zeleny, "Trump Furious over Leak of Warning to Not Congratulate Putin," *CNN*, March 22, 2018.
13. Philip Bump, "There's Still Little Evidence That Russia's 2016 Social Media Efforts Did Much of Anything," *Washington Post*, December 28, 2017. For an opposing perspective stressing the Kremlin's targeted message in battleground states, see Kathleen Hall Jamieson, *Cyberwar: How Russia Helped Elect Trump* (New York: Oxford University Press, 2018).
14. Jeremy Herb and Manu Raju, "House Republicans Break with Intelligence Community on Russia," *CNN*, March 12, 2018.
15. "Despite Mueller's Push, House Republicans Declare No Evidence of Collusion," *New York Times*, March 12, 2018.
16. Scott McConnell, "Has Donald Trump Betrayed His Base?," *National Interest*, September 2017.
17. Paul Sunders, "Donald Trump's Foreign Policy: Working with Russia from a Position of Strength," *Valdai Club*, March 2017.
18. Vladimir Frolov, "Why Russia Won't Cave to Western Demands," *Moscow Times*, May 3, 2017.
19. As cited in Aaron Maté, "What We've Learned in Year 1 of Russiagate," *The Nation*, February 9, 2018.
20. Jenna Lifhits, "John Bolton's Long History as a Russia Hawk," *Weekly Standard*, March 22, 2018.
21. See, for example, Burke, "If You Weren't Already Worried"; "Tough Action on Russia, at Last, but More Is Needed," editorial, *New York Times*, March 27, 2018; "The Russian Expulsions Are a Good First Step. But Only a First Step," editorial, *Washington Post*, March 27, 2018.
22. Janusz Bugajski, "Fight Putin with Fire," *Wall Street Journal*, February 14, 2018 Others recommended a strategy of deterrence with clearly defined consequences for adversarial actions (Alina Polyakova, "The Next Russian Attack Will Be Far Worse Than Bots and Trolls," *Lawfare*, March 20, 2018).
23. "Why Is Trump So Afraid of Russia?," editorial, *New York Times*, March 22, 2018.
24. Walter Russell Mead, "Trump Isn't Sounding Like a Russian Mole," *American Interest*, February 24, 2017, https://www.the-american-interest.com/2017/02/24/trump-isnt-sounding-like-a-russian-mole/.

25. Virgil, "The Real Siberian Candidate and the Deep State," *Breitbart*, December 19, 2016; Sean Hannity, "The Deep State's Massive Effort to Destroy Trump," *Fox News*, June 16, 2017.
26. Anna Popkova, "'Putin Is Playing Chess and I Think We Are Playing Marbles.' Vladimir Putin's 'Soft Power' and the American Right," *International Communication Gazette*, April 2017).
27. Ibid., 444, 446.
28. Leonid Bershidsky, "Putin Starts to Win American Minds, If Not Hearts," *Bloomberg*, January 18, 2017. For an analysis of Putin's global appeal, see Greg Simons, "Aspects of Putin's Appeal to International Public," *Global Affairs* 1 no. 2 (2015): 205–08.
29. Marlene Laruelle, "Russian and American Far Right Connections: Confluence, Not Influence," *PONARS Policy Memo*, March 12, 2018.
30. Glasser, "Our Putin."
31. Gary Leupp, "What If There Was No Collusion?," *CounterPunch*, March 16, 2018. For a similar argument, see also Natylie Baldwin, "Acceptable Bigotry and Scapegoating of Russia," *Consortiumnews*, March 15, 2018.
32. Justin Raimondo, "The New Cold War Is Here," *Antiwar.com*, March 5, 2018.
33. Glenn Greenwald and Zaid Jilani, "With Latest Syria Threats, Trump Continues to Be More Confrontational toward Russia Than Obama Was," *The Intercept*, April 11, 2018.
34. Ibid.
35. Ben Norton and Glenn Greenwald, "Washington Post Disgracefully Promotes a McCarthyite Blacklist from a New, Hidden, and Very Shady Group," *The Intercept*, November 26, 2016.
36. Burke, "If You Weren't Already Worried."
37. Masha Gessen, "The Fundamental Uncertainty of Mueller's Russia Indictments," *New Yorker*, February 20, 2018.
38. Ibid.
39. Blake Hounshell, "Confessions of a Russiagate Skeptic," *Politico*, February 18, 2018.
40. Stephen Lee Myers, "Was the 2016 Election a Game of 'Russian Roulette'?," *New York Times*, March 14, 2018.
41. WIN/Gallup International End of Year 2013, http://www.wingia.com/web/files/richeditor/filemanager/291213_EOY_release_2013_for_MENA_and_Africa_-_final.pdf.
42. Jeffrey M. Jones, "Record-High 77% of Americans Perceive Nation as Divided," *Gallup*, November 21, 2016, http://www.gallup.com/poll/197828/record-high-americans-perceive-nation-divided.aspx.
43. Some scholars relate such polarization to the United States' belated democratization and the emergence of a divided Congress in the 1970s (Robert Mickey, Steven Levitsky, and Lucan Ahmad Way, "Is America Still Safe for Democracy?," *Foreign Affairs*, April 17, 2017).

44. Kristen Bialik, "Putin Remains Overwhelmingly Unpopular in the United States," *Pew Research Center*, March 26, 2018, http://www.pewresearch.org/fact-tank/2018/03/26/putin-remains-overwhelmingly-unpopular-in-the-united-states/.
45. "Clinton, Trump Clash In Bitter Debate, Spar over Russian Hacking," *Radio Free Europe / Radio Liberty*, Sep 27, 2016 http://www.rferl.org/a/clinton-trump-face-off-first-us-presidential-debate-november-election/28015528.html.
46. Michael Crowley and Tyler Pager, "Trump Urges Russia to Hack Clinton's Email," *Politico*, July 27, 2016.
47. Ginger Gibson, "Clinton Accuses Trump of Being Putin's 'Puppet,'" *Reuters*, October 20, 2017.
48. Haliman Abdullah, "Hillary Clinton Singles Out Putin, Comey in Election Loss," *NBC News*, December 16, 2016, http://www.nbcnews.com/news/us-news/hillary-clinton-singles-out-putin-comey-election-loss-n696991.
49. Hillary Rodham Clinton, *Hard Choices: A Memoir* (New York: Simon and Schuster, 2014), 2.
50. Barack Obama, Transcript: Obama's remarks on Russia, NSA at the Hague on March 25, 2014, https://www.washingtonpost.com/world/national-security/transcript-obamas-remarks-on-russia-nsa-at-the-hague-on-march-25/2014/03/25/412950ca-b445-11e3-8cb6-284052554d74_story.html?utm_term=.d4dd43fd2abf.
51. Gabriel Debenedetti, "Liberal Group Launches 'Moscow Project' to Pressure Trump," *Politco.com*, February 22, 2017.
52. Evan Osnos, David Remnick, and Joshua Yaffa, "Trump, Putin, and the New Cold War," *New Yorker*, March 6, 2017.
53. Morgan Chalfant, "Democrats Step Up Calls That Russian Hack Was Act of War," *The Hill*, March 26, 2017.
54. Petra Cahill, "Dick Cheney: Russian Election Interference Possibly 'Act of War,'" March 28, 2017, http://www.nbcnews.com/politics/white-house/dick-cheney-russian-election-interference-could-be-seen-act-war-n739391.
55. Chalfant, "Democrats Step Up Calls."
56. Gareth Porter, "How 'New Cold Warriors' Cornered Trump," *Consortiumnews.com*, February 25, 2017.
57. Following the resignation of Trump's national security advisor, Michael Flynn, over not disclosing his meeting with Kislyak, the Kremlin recalled him and appointed Mikhail Antonov as new ambassador to the United States.
58. Richard Hofstadter, "The Paranoid Style in American Politics," *Harper's*, November 1964, http://harpers.org/archive/1964/11/the-paranoid-style-in-american-politics/.
59. According to some sources, Saudi Arabia donated more than $10 million to the Clinton Foundation before the elections (Amy Chozick and Steve Eder, "Foundation Ties Bedevil Hillary Clinton's Presidential Campaign," *New York*

Times, August 20, 2016). On the Ukraine connection, see Kenneth P. Vogel and David Stern, "Ukrainian Efforts to Sabotage Trump Backfire," *Politico*, January 2017.

60. Justin Raimondo, "Rush to Judgment: The Evidence That the Russians Hacked the DNC Is Collapsing," *Antiwar.com*, March 24, 2017; Leonid Bershidsky, "Why Some U.S. Ex-Spies Don't Buy the Russia Story, *Bloomberg*, August 10, 2017.
61. Jesse Walker, "Is the Trump-Russia Story an Octopus or Spaghetti?," *Los Angeles Times*, March 24, 2017.
62. Masha Gessen, "Don't Fight Their Lies with Lies of Your Own," *New York Times*, March 26, 2017.
63. Maté, "What We've Learned."
64. Mark Lawrence Schrad, "Vladimir Putin Isn't a Supervillain," *Foreign Policy*, March 2, 2017.
65. Arjun Kapur and Simon Saradzhyan, "For Russia and America, Election Inference Is Nothing New: 25 Stories," *Russia Matters*, March 22, 2017.
66. George Kennan, "America and the Russian Future," *Foreign Affairs*, April 1951.
67. Julien Nocetti, "Cyber Power," in Tsygankov, *Handbook of Russian Foreign Policy*; Brandon Valeriano, Benjamin Jensen, and Ryan C. Maness, *Cyber Strategy: The Evolving Character of Power and Coercion* (New York: Oxford University Press, 2018).
68. Andrei Tsygankov, "Russia's (Limited) Information War on the West," *Public Diplomacy*, June 5, 2017; Charles Ziegler, "International Dimensions of Electoral Processes: Russia, the USA, and the 2016 elections," *International Politics*, October 2017.
69. Nocetti, "Cyber Power," 190–91.

Chapter 6

1. For instance, speaking at the St. Petersburg Economic Forum, Putin was critical of the institution of superdelegates in the United States' system and implied that on two occasions election results were stolen: "Twice in the history of the United States, presidents were elected by the majority of delegates, yet these delegates represented a minority of voters. Is this a democracy?" (Plenary Meeting of St. Petersburg Economic Forum, June 17, 2016, http://www.kremlin.ru/events/president/news/52178).
2. "A Colder War with Russia?," Editorial, *New York Times*, March 31, 2018.
3. "On His Way Out, McMaster Tells the Truth. Trump Should Listen," editorial, *Washington Post*, April 5, 2018.
4. Previously, such views in the media were less frequent and viewed as unusual. For instance, in 2008, a professor of Diplomatic Academy, Igor' Panarin, forecast the probable disintegration of the United States into six parts in 2010—a view that was well publicized in the Western media as well, perhaps because

it was so unusual ("As If Things Were Not Bad Enough, Russian Professor Predicts End of U.S.," *Wall Street Journal*, December 29, 2008).
5. Peter Rutland, "Trump, Putin, and the Future of US-Russian Relations," *Slavic Review*, August 2017.
6. For a detailed analysis of Russian coverage of Trump, see Laurence Bogoslaw, ed., *Russians on Trump: Press Coverage and Commentary* (Minneapolis: East View Press, 2018).
7. Anatol Lieven, "A Poisonous Giant Russian Squid Ate Trump's Brain!," *Valdai Discussion Club*, April 7, 2017.
8. "Americans, Particularly Democrats, Dislike Russia," *Gallup Poll*, March 5, 2018, http://news.gallup.com/poll/228479/americans-particularly-democrats-dislike-russia.aspx.
9. According to a poll conducted in December 2017, 81% of Russians agreed with the statement, "The USA seeks to limit Russia's international influence and power" (Stepan Goncharov, "Conflicting Views: How the Russian Public Perceives Relations with America," *Intersection*, February 13, 2018).
10. Legvold, *Return to Cold War*.
11. Stephen M. Walt, "The Collapse of the Liberal World Order," *Foreign Policy*, June 26, 2016.
12. E. H. Carr, *The Twenty Years' Crisis, 1919–1939: An Introduction to the Study of International Relations* (New York: Harper, 1964), 236.
13. Ido Oren, *Our Enemy and US: America's Rivalries and the Making of Political Science* (Ithaca, NY: Cornell University Press, 2002).
14. Andrew Wilson, *Virtual Democracy: Faking Democracy in the Post-Soviet World* (New Haven: Yale University Press, 2005); Pomerantsev, *Nothing Is True*.
15. For some analyses of such public pressures, see John Howes Gleason, *The Genesis of Russophobia in Great Britain: A Study of the Interaction of Policy and Opinion* (Cambridge, MA: Harvard University Press, 1950); Astrid S. Tuminez, *Russian Nationalism since 1856: Ideology and the Making of Foreign Policy* (Lanham, MD: Rowman & Littlefield, 2000); Edward D. Mansfield and Jack Snyder, *Electing to Fight: Why Emerging Democracies Go to War* (Cambridge, MA: MIT Press, 2005); Misha Glenny, *The Balkans: Nationalism, War, and the Great Powers, 1804–2011* (New York: Penguin, 2012).
16. For analysis of the Islamist ideological challenge, see John M. Owen IV, *Confronting Political Islam: Six Lessons from the West's Past* (Princeton, NJ: Princeton University Press, 2016).
17. Joseph Nye, *Bound to Lead: The Changing Nature of American Power* (New York: Basic Books, 1990); see also his *Soft Power*.
18. In response, French foreign minister Dominique de Villepin had to tone down differences with Washington by calling on the United States "not to oppose one Europe to another while everyone sees we defend the same principles: firmness toward Iraq and the will to find a solution to the crisis in the

framework of the United Nations" (as cited in Pepe Escobar, "Listening to Europe," *Asia Times On Line*, February 1, 2003).
19. John Rogin, "Trump to Unveil Plans for an 'Arab NATO' in Saudi Arabia," *Washington Post*, May 17, 2017.
20. Henry Kissinger, *World Order* (New York: Penguin, 2014), 371.

BIBLIOGRAPHY

Allison, R. 2013. *Russia, the West, and Military Intervention*. New York: Oxford University Press.

Anschel, Eugene, ed. 1975. *The American Image of Russia: 1775–1917*. New York: Ungar.

Applebaum, A. and E. Lucas. 2015. "Putin's News Network of Lies Is Just the Start." *Newsweek.com*, August 11.

Arnold, R. 2016. *Russian Nationalism and Ethnic Violence: Symbolic Violence, Lynching, Pogrom and Massacre*. London: Routledge.

Arutunyan, A. 2014. *The Putin Mystique: Inside Russia's Power Cult*. London: Olive Brunch.

Baker, P. and S. Glasser. 2005. *Kremlin Rising: Vladimir Putin's Russia and the End of Revolution*. New York: Simon and Schuster.

Baldwin, N. 2018. "Acceptable Bigotry and Scapegoating of Russia." *Consortiumnews*, March 15.

Batalov, E. Ya., V. Yu. Zhuravleva, and K. V. Khozinskaya. 2009. *Rychashchiy medved' na "dikov Vostoke". (Obrazu sovremennoi Rossiyi v rabotakh sovremennykh amerikanskikh avtorov)*. Moscow: Rosspen.

Bayulgen, O. and E. Arbatli. 2013. "Cold War Redux in US-Russia Relations? The Effects of US Media Framing and Public Opinion of the 2008 Russia-Georgia War." *Communist and Post-Communist Studies* 46: 513–27.

Bennett, W. L. 1990. "Toward a Theory of Press-State Relations in the United States." *Journal of Communication* 40: 103–23.

Bennett, W. L. 2003. "A Semi-independent Press: Government Control and Journalistic Autonomy in the Political Construction of News." *Political Communication* 20: 381–414.

Berger, A. A. 1997. *Narratives in Popular Culture, Media, and Everyday Life*. London: Sage.

Berman, I. 2014. "Wanted: A Real War of Ideas with Russia." *National Interest*, July 3.

Bershidsky, L. 2017. "Why Some U.S. Ex-Spies Don't Buy the Russia Story." *Bloomberg*, August 10.

Bershidsky, L. 2017. "Putin Starts to Win American Minds, If Not Hearts." *Bloomberg*, January 18.

Bialik, K. 2018. "Putin Remains Overwhelmingly Unpopular in the United States." *Pew Research Center*, March 26.

Bogoslaw, L., ed. 2018. *Russians on Trump: Press Coverage and Commentary*. Minneapolis: East View Press.

Bowker, M. 2006. "Western Views of the Chechen Conflict." In R. Sakwa, ed., *Chechnya: From Past to Future*. London: Anthem Press.

Boyd-Barrett, O. 2016. *Western Mainstream Media and the Ukraine Crisis: A Study in Conflict Propaganda*. London: Routledge.

Braithwaite, R. 2002. *Across the Moscow River: The World Turned Upside Down*. New Haven: Yale University Press.

Bronfenbrenner, U. 1961. "The Mirror Image in Soviet-American Relations: A Social Psychologist's Report." *Journal of Social Issues* 17, no. 3: 45–56.

Brudny, Y. M. 2000. *Reinventing Russia Russian Nationalism and the Soviet State, 1953–1991*. Cambridge, MA: Harvard University Press.

Brzezinski, Z. 1989. *The Grand Failure: The Birth and Death of Communism in the Twentieth Century*. New York: Collier Books.

Brzezinski, Z. 1997. "A Geostrategy for Eurasia." *Foreign Affairs* 76, no. 5: 50–64.

Buchanan, P. 2018. "Time to Get Over the Russophobia." *American Conservative*, March 8.

Bugajski, J. 2018. "Fight Putin with Fire." *Wall Street Journal*, February 14.

Cacciatore, M. A. and D. A. Scheufele. 2016. "The End of Framing as We Know It . . . and the Future of Media Effects." *Mass Communication and Society* 19, no. 1: 7–23.

Campbell, D. 1992. *Writing Security: United States Foreign Policy and the Politics of Identity*. Minneapolis: University of Minnesota Press.

Carden, J. 2015. "Neo-McCarthyism and the US Media." *The Nation*, May 20.

Carden, J. 2016. "Uncle Sam Got a Shiny New Propaganda Bullhorn for Christmas: A New Partnership Is Turning Radio Free Europe into an Anti-Russia Propaganda Machine." *The Nation*, January 5.

Carr, E. H. 1964. *The Twenty Years' Crisis, 1919–1939: An Introduction to the Study of International Relations*. New York: Harper.

Castells, M. 2007. "Communication, Power and Counter-power in the Network Society." *International Journal of Communication* 1: 238–66.

Chebankova, E. 2014. "Contemporary Russian Liberalism." *Post-Soviet Affairs* 30, no. 5: 341–69.

Chebankova, E. 2016. "Contemporary Russian Conservatism." *Post-Soviet Affairs* 32, no. 1: 28–54.

Chebankova, E. 2017. "Russia's Idea of the Multipolar World Order." *Post-Soviet Affairs* 33, no. 3: 217–34. https://www.tandfonline.com/doi/abs/10.1080/1060586X.2017.1293394.

Chen, A. 2016. "The Propaganda about Russian Propaganda." *New Yorker*, December 1.

Cheney, R. 2006. *Vice President's Remarks at the 2006 Vilnius Conference.* Vilnius, Lithuania: The White House, Office of the Vice President. May 4. http://georgewbush-whitehouse.archives.gov/news/releases/2006/05/20060504-1.html.

Clinton, H. R. 2014. *Hard Choices: A Memoir.* New York: Simon and Schuster.

Clover, Charles. 2016. *Black Wind, White Snow: The Rise of Russia's New Nationalism.* New Haven: Yale University Press.

Clunan, A. L. 2009. *The Social Construction of Russia's Resurgence: Aspirations, Identity, and Security Interests.* Baltimore: John Hopkins University Press.

Cohen, J. L. 2012. *Globalization and Sovereignty: Rethinking Legality, Legitimacy, and Constitutionalism.* Cambridge: Cambridge University Press.

Cohen, S. F. 2001. *The Failed Crusade: America and the Tragedy of Post-Communist Russia.* New York: Norton.

Cohen, S. F. 2012. "Stop the Pointless Demonization of Putin." *Reuters,* May 7.

Cohen, S. F. 2018. *Why Cold War Again? How America Lost Post-Soviet Russia.* London: I.B. Tauris.

Combs, J. A. 1997. *The History of American Foreign Policy.* London: Routledge.

Cottam, M. L. 1994. *Images and Intervention: U.S. Policies in Latin America.* Pittsburgh: University of Pittsburgh Press.

Cuhadar, E. and B. Dayton. 2011. "The Social Psychology of Identity and Intergroup Conflict." *International Studies Review* 12: 273–93.

Dalby, S. 1988. "Geopolitical Discourse: The Soviet Union as Other." *Alternatives: Global, Local, Political* 13 (October): 415–42.

Deyermond, R. 2012. "The Republican Challenge to Obama's Russia Policy." *Survival* 54, no. 5: 67–92.

Deyermond, R. 2012. "Reset or Disconnected? Russian Media and Internet Freedom as a Site of Contestation in US-Russia Relations and US Domestic Politics." Paper presented at the International Studies Association Annual Meeting, April 1–4, San Diego.

Diesen, G. 2018. *The Decay of Western Civilization and Resurgence of Russia.* London: Routledge.

Dobriansky, P. J. 2014. "U.S. Needs a Strong Moral Narrative to Combat Putin." *Washington Post,* May 24.

Duncan, P. J. S. 2013. "Russia, the West and the 2007–2008 Electoral Cycle: Did the Kremlin Really Fear a 'Coloured Revolution'?" *Europe-Asia Studies* 65, no. 1: 1–25.

Dunn, J. A. 2014. "Lottizzazione Russian Style: Russia's Two-Tier Media System." *Europe-Asia Studies* 66, no. 9: 1425–51.

Dvoichenko-Markov, E. 1950. "Jefferson and the Russian Decembrists." *American Slavic and East European Review* 9, no. 3: 162–68.

Elders, C. 1999. "Synchronization of Issue Agendas in News and Editorials of the Prestige Press in Germany." *Communications* 24, no. 3: 301–28.

English, R. D. 2017. "Russia, Trump, and a New Détente." *Foreign Affairs,* March 10.

Entman, R. M. 2009. *Projections of Power: Framing News, Public Opinion, and U.S. Foreign Policy*. Chicago: University of Chicago Press.

Feklyunina, V. 2012. "Constructing Russophobia." In R. Taras, ed., *Russia's Identity in International Relations: Images, Perceptions, Misperceptions*. London: Routledge.

Feklyunina, V. 2015. "Soft Power and Identity: Russia, Ukraine and the 'Russian World(s).'" *European Journal of International Relations* 22, no. 4: 773–96.

Flikke, G. 2017. "The Sword of Damocles: State Governability in Putin's Third Term." *Problems of Post-Communism*. https://www.tandfonline.com/doi/full/10.1080/10758216.2017.1291308.

Foglesong, D. 2007. *The American Mission and the "Evil Empire": The Crusade for a "Free Russia" since 1881*. Cambridge: Cambridge University Press.

Formisano, R. P. 2015. *Plutocracy in America: How Increasing Inequality Destroys the Middle Class and Exploits the Poor*. Baltimore: John Hopkins University Press.

Forsberg, T. and H. Smith. 2016. "Russian Cultural Statecraft in the Eurasian Space." *Problems of Post-Communism* 63, no. 3: 129–34.

Forsythe, D. P. and P. C. McMahon. 2017. *American Exceptionalism Reconsidered: U.S. Foreign Policy, Human Rights, and World Order*. London: Routledge.

Fried, D. 2017. "Russia's Back-to-the-80s Foreign Policy." *The Atlantic*, August 2.

Friedrichs, J. 2016. "An Intercultural Theory of International Relations: How Self-Worth Underlies Politics among Nations." *International Theory* 8, no. 1: 63–96.

Fukuyama, F. 1989. "The End of History?" *National Interest* 16 (Summer): 3–18.

Gaufman, L. 2017. *Security Threat and Public Perceptions: Digital Russia and the Ukraine Crisis*. London: Palgrave.

Gessen, M. 2017. "Don't Fight Their Lies with Lies of Your Own." *New York Times*, March 26.

Gessen, M. 2018. "The Fundamental Uncertainty of Mueller's Russia Indictments." *New Yorker*, February 20.

Giannone, D. 2010. "Political and Ideological Aspects in the Measurement of Democracy: The Freedom House Case." *Democratization* 17, no. 1: 68–97.

Gibson, G. 2017. "Clinton Accuses Trump of Being Putin's 'puppet.'" *Reuters*, October 20.

Glasser, S. B. 2017. "Our Putin." *New York Times*, February 18.

Gleason, J. H. 1950. *The Genesis of Russophobia in Great Britain: A Study of the Interaction of Policy and Opinion*. Cambridge, MA: Harvard University Press.

Glenny, M. 2012. *The Balkans: Nationalism, War, and the Great Powers, 1804–2011*. New York: Penguin.

Godzimirski, J. M. 2015. "What Makes Dialogue and Diplomacy Work or Not? Russia-Georgia and Russia-Ukraine." In Pernille Rieker and H. Thune, eds., *Dialogue and Conflict Resolution: Potential and Limits*. Burlington, VT: Ashgate.

Goldgeier, J. and M. McFaul. 2003. *Power and Purpose: U.S. Policy toward Russia after the Cold War.* Washington, DC: Brookings.

Goncharov, S. 2018. "Conflicting Views: How the Russian Public Perceives Relations with America." *Intersection*, February 13.

Good, Jane E. 1982. "America and the Russian Revolutionary Movement, 1888–1905." *Russian Review* 41, no. 3: 273–87.

Greenwald, G. 2017. "Yet Another Major Russia Story Falls Apart. Is Skepticism Permissible Yet?" *The Intercept*, September 28.

Greenwald, G. and Z. Jilani. 2018. "With Latest Syria Threats, Trump Continues to Be More Confrontational toward Russia Than Obama Was." *The Intercept*, April 11.

Guillory, S. 2017. "A Genealogy of American Russophobia." *In Russia*, April 17.

Guzzini, S., ed. 2012. *The Return of Geopolitics in Europe? Social Mechanisms and Foreign Policy Identity Crises.* Cambridge: Cambridge University Press.

Hafez, K. 2007. *The Myth of Media Globalization.* Cambridge: Polity Press.

Hale, H. 2010. "Eurasian Politics as Hybrid Regimes: The Case of Putin's Russia." *Journal of Eurasian Studies* 1, no. 1: 33–41.

Hale, H. 2014. *Patronal Politics: Eurasian Regime Dynamics in Comparative Perspective.* Cambridge: Cambridge University Press.

Hall, T. H. 2015. *Emotional Diplomacy: Official Emotion on the International Stage.* Ithaca, NY: Cornell University Press.

Hannity, S. 2017. "The Deep State's Massive Effort to Destroy Trump." *Fox News*, June 16.

Hart, G. 2007. "Don't Lose Russia." *National Interest*, March–April.

Hayden, G. 2012. *The Rhetoric of Soft Power: Public Diplomacy in Global Contexts.* New York: Lexington Books.

Herman, E. S. and N. Chomsky. 1988. *Manufacturing Consent.* New York: Pantheon.

Herrmann, R. 1985. *Perceptions and Behavior in Soviet Foreign Policy.* Pittsburgh: University of Pittsburgh Press.

Hofstadter, R. 1964. "The Paranoid Style in American Politics." *Harper's*, November. http://harpers.org/archive/1964/11/the-paranoid-style-in-american-politics/.

Hopf, T. 2002. *Social Construction of International Politics: Identities and Foreign Policies, Moscow, 1955 and 1999.* Ithaca, NY: Cornell University Press.

Hounshell, B. 2018. "Confessions of a Russiagate Skeptic." *Politico*, February 18.

Inayatullah, N. and D. Blaney. 2004. *International Relations and the Problem of Difference.* London: Routledge.

Izadi, F. and H. Saqhave-Biria. 2007. "A Discourse Analysis of Elite American Newspaper Editorials." *Journal of Communication Inquiry* 31, no. 2: 140–65.

Jamieson, K. H. 2018. *Cyberwar: How Russia Helped Elect Trump.* Oxford University Press.

Jeffery, R. 2014. *Reason and Emotion in International Ethics.* Cambridge: Cambridge University Press.

Jones, J. M. 2015. "Confidence in U.S. Institutions Still below Historical Norms." *Gallup*, June 15.
Kanet, R. E., ed. 2017. *The Russian Challenge to the European Security Environment*. New York: Palgrave.
Kapur, A. and S. Saradzhyan. 2017. "For Russia and America, Election Inference Is Nothing New: 25 Stories." *Russia Matters*, March 22.
Katchanovski, I. 2016. "The Far Right in Ukraine during the 'Euromaidan' and the War in Donbas." September 2. https://ssrn.com/abstract=2832203 or http://dx.doi.org/10.2139/ssrn.2832203.
Katchanovski, I. and A. R. Morley. 2012. "The Politics of U.S. Television Coverage of Post-Communist Countries." *Problems of Post-Communism* 59, no. 1: 15–30.
Keating, V. C. and K. Kaczmarska. 2017. "Conservative Soft Power: Liberal Soft Power Bias and the 'Hidden' Attraction of Russia." *Journal of International Relations and Development*. doi: 10.1057/s41268-017-0100-6.
Kennan, G. 1951. "America and the Russian Future." *Foreign Affairs*.
Kennedy, D. 2014. "Who's Afraid of Russia Today? Is RT, Formerly Russia Today, Really as Dangerous or as Effective as Its Critics Claim?" *www.opendemocracy.net*, December 5.
Kinnvall, C. and J. Mitzen. 2016. "An Introduction to the Special Issue: Ontological Securities in World Politics." *Cooperation & Conflict*, July 11.
Kissinger, H. 2014. "To Settle the Ukraine Crisis, Start at the End." *Washington Post*, March 5.
Kissinger, H. 2014. *World Order*. New York: Penguin Books.
Kolstø, P. and H. Blakkisrud, eds. 2015. *The New Russian Nationalism: Imperialism, Ethnicity, and Authoritarianism, 2000–15*. Manchester: Manchester University Press.
Kortunov, S. 2002. "Rossiysko-amerikanskoye partnerstvo." *Mezhdunarodnaya zhizn'* 2: 42–69.
Kramer. D. J. 2010. "America's Silence Makes Us Complicit in Russia's Crimes." *Washington Post*, September 20.
Kramer, D. J. 2015. "The West Should Take on the Putin P.R. Machine." *Washington Post*, October 25.
Krasheninnikova, V. 2013. *Rossiya-America: kholodnaya voina kul'tur*. Moscow: Yevropa.
Krauthammer, C. 1991. "The Unipolar Moment." *Foreign Affairs* 70, no. 1: 23–33.
Krebs, R. R. 2015. "How Dominant Narratives Rise and Fall: Military Conflict, Politics, and the Cold War Consensus." *International Organization*, 69, no. 4: 809–45.
Kristof, N. 2017. "There's a Smell of Treason in the Air." *New York Times*, March 23.
Krugman, P. 2016. "Donald Trump, the Siberian Candidate." *New York Times*, July 22.
Kurilla, I. 2016. "Abolition of Serfdom in Russia and American Newspaper and Journal Opinion." In W. B. Whisenhunt and N. E. Saul, eds., *New Perspectives on Russian-American Relations*. London: Routledge.

Lambert, F. *The Founding Fathers and the Place of Religion in America.* Princeton, NJ: Princeton University Press.
Laruelle, M., ed. 2009. *Russian Nationalism and the National Reassertion of Russia.* London: Routledge.
Laruelle, M. 2018. "Russian and American Far Right Connections: Confluence, Not Influence." *PONARS Policy Memo,* March 12.
Lawrence, P. 2016. "The Perils of Russophobia." *The Nation,* December 29.
Le, E. 2010. *Editorials and the Power of Media: Interweaving of Socio-cultural Identities.* Amsterdam: John Benjamins.
Lebow, R. N. 2003. *The Tragic Vision of Politics: Ethics, Interests and Orders.* Cambridge: Cambridge University Press.
Lebow, R. N. 2016. *National Identities and International Relations.* Cambridge: Cambridge University Press.
Legvold, R. 2001. "Russia's Unreformed Foreign Policy." *Foreign Affairs,* September–October.
Legvold, R., ed. 2007. *Russian Foreign Policy in the Twenty-First Century and the Shadow of the Past.* New York: Columbia University Press.
Legvold, R. 2016. *Return to Cold War.* Cambridge: Polity Press.
Leupp, G. 2018. "What If There Was No Collusion?" *CounterPunch,* March 16.
Lieven, A. 2000. "Against Russophobia." *World Policy Journal* 17, no. 4: 25–32.
Lieven, A. 2004. *America Right or Wrong: Anatomy of American Nationalism.* New York: Oxford University Press.
Lieven, A. 2017. "A Poisonous Giant Russian Squid Ate Trump's Brain!" *Valdai Discussion Club,* April 7.
Linde, F. 2016. "The Civilizational Turn in Russian Political Discourse: From Pan-Europeanism to Civilizational Distinctiveness." *Russian Review* 75, no. 4: 604–25.
Lucarelli, S. and I. Manners, eds. 2006. *Values and Principles in European Union Foreign Policy.* London: Routledge.
Lucas, E. 2008. *The New Cold War: Putin's Russia and the Threat to the West.* London: Palgrave.
Lusk, A. 2018. "Moving Beyond the CNN Effect or Stuck in the Middle? How Relational Sociology Remaps Media and Security Studies." *International Studies Review,* April 12. https://doi.org/10.1093/isr/viy003.
Lynch, M. 1999. *State Interests and Public Spheres.* New York: Columbia University Press.
MacKinnon, M. 2007. *The New Cold War: Revolutions, Rigged Elections and Pipeline Politics in the Former Soviet Union.* Toronto: Random House.
Mäkinen, S. 2016. "In Search of the Status of an Educational Great Power? Analysis of Russia's Educational Diplomacy Discourse." *Problems of Post-Communism* 63, no. 3: 183–96.
Mannheim, K. [1936] 2015. *Ideology and Utopia: An Introduction to the Sociology of Knowledge.* Eastford: Martino Fine Books.

Mansfield, E. D. and J. Snyder. 2005. *Electing to Fight: Why Emerging Democracies Go to War*. Cambridge, MA: MIT Press.

Maréchal, N. 2017. "Networked Authoritarianism and the Geopolitics of Information: Understanding Russian Internet Policy." *Media and Communication* 5: 29–41.

Markwica, R. 2018. *Emotional Choices: How the Logic of Affect Shapes Coercive Diplomacy*. New York: Oxford University Press.

Marshall, M. G. 2014. *Political Regime Characteristics and Transitions, 1800–2013*. Polity IV. http://www.systemicpeace.org/polity/polity4x.htm.

Maté, A. 2018. "What We've Learned in Year 1 of Russiagate." *The Nation*, February 9.

McCarthy, D. 2011. "Open Networks and the Open Door: American Foreign Policy and the Narration of the Internet." *Foreign Policy Analysis* 7: 89–111.

McDermott, R., N. Wernimont, and Ch. Koopman. 2011. "Applying Psychology to International Studies: Challenges and Opportunities in Examining Traumatic Stress." *International Studies Perspectives* 12: 119–35.

McFaul, M. 2008. "Russia: More Stick, Less Carrot." *Hoover Digest* 1: 43.

McFaul, M. 2014. "Confronting Putin's Russia." *New York Times*, March 24.

Mead, W. R. 2002. *Special Providence: American Foreign Policy and How It Changed the World*. London: Routledge.

Mead, W. R. 2017. "Trump Isn't Sounding Like a Russian Mole." *American Interest*, February 24. https://www.the-american-interest.com/2017/02/24/trump-isnt-sounding-like-a-russian-mole/.

Mearsheimer, J. 2011. *Why Leaders Lie: The Truth about Lying in International Politics*. New York: Oxford University Press.

Mercer, J. 2010. "Emotional Beliefs." *International Organization* 64: 1–34.

Mettan, G. 2017. *Creating Russophobia: From the Great Religious Schism to Anti-Putin Hysteria*. New York: Clarity Press.

Mickey, R., S. Levitsky, and L. A. Way. 2017. "Is America Still Safe for Democracy?" *Foreign Affairs*, April 17.

Mickiewicz, E. 2009. *Television, Power, and the Public in Russia*. Cambridge: Cambridge University Press.

Miskimmon, A., B. O'Loughlin, and L. Roselle. 2013. *Strategic Narratives: Communication Power and the New World Order*. London: Routledge.

Myers, S. L. 2016. *The New Russian Tsar: The Rise and Reign of Vladimir Putin*. New York: Vintage.

Myers, S. L. 2018. "Was the 2016 Election a Game of 'Russian Roulette'?" *New York Times*, March 14.

Nocetti, J. 2018. "Cyber Power." In A. P. Tsygankov, ed., *The Routledge Handbook of Russian Foreign Policy*. London: Routledge.

Norton, B. and G. Greenwald. 2016. "Washington Post Disgracefully Promotes a McCarthyite Blacklist from a New, Hidden, and Very Shady Group." *The Intercept*, November 26.

Nye, J. 1990. *Bound to Lead: The Changing Nature of American Power*. New York: Basic Books.
Nye, J. 2004. *Soft Power: The Means to Success in World Politics*. New York: Public Affairs.
Oates, S. 2007. "The Neo-Soviet Model of the Media." *Europe-Asia Studies* 59, no. 8: 1279–97.
Obama, B. 2014. Transcript: Obama's remarks on Russia, NSA at the Hague on March 25. https://www.washingtonpost.com/world/national-security/transcript-obamas-remarks-on-russia-nsa-at-the-hague-on-march-25/2014/03/25/412950ca-b445-11e3-8cb6-284052554d74_story.html?utm_term=.d4dd43fd2abf.
Oren, I. 2002. *Our Enemy and US: America's Rivalries and the Making of Political Science*. Ithaca, NY: Cornell University Press.
Ortmann, S. and J. Heathershaw. 2012. "Conspiracy Theories in the Post-Soviet Space." *Russian Review* 71, no. 4: 551–64.
Osgood, K. A. 2002. "Hearts and Minds: The Unconventional Cold War." *Journal of Cold War Studies* 4, no. 2: 85–107.
Oslon, A., ed. 2001. *Amerika: vzglyad iz Rossiyi*. Moscow: Institut Fonda "Obschestvennoye mneniye."
Osnos, E., D. Remnick, and J. Yaffa. 2017. "Trump, Putin, and the New Cold War." *New Yorker*, March 6.
Ostrovsky, A. 2015. *The Invention of Russia: From Gorbachev's Freedom to Putin's War*. New York: Random House.
Owen, J. M., IV 2010. *The Clash of Ideas in World Politics: Transnational Networks, States, and Regime Change, 1510–2010*. Princeton, NJ: Princeton University Press.
Owen, J. M., IV 2016. *Confronting Political Islam: Six Lessons from the West's Past*. Princeton, NJ: Princeton University Press.
Parry, R. 2017. "Protecting the Shaky Russia-gate Narrative." *Consortium News*, December 15.
Petro, N. 1995. *The Rebirth of Russian Democracy: An Interpretation of Political Culture*. Cambridge, MA: Harvard University Press.
Petrov, N. M. Lipman, and H. Hale. 2013. "Three Dilemmas of Hybrid Regime Governance: Russia from Putin to Putin." *Post-Soviet Affairs* 26, no. 1: 1–26.
Pfaff, W. 1991. "Redefining World Power." *Foreign Affairs* 70, no. 1: 34–48.
Pipes, R. 1997. "Is Russia Still an Enemy?." *Foreign Affairs* 76, no. 5: 65–78.
Pomerantsev, P. 2014. *Nothing Is True and Everything Is Possible*. New York: Public Affairs.
Pomerantsev, P. 2015. "The Kremlin's Information War." *Journal of Democracy* 25, no. 4: 40–50.
Ponarin, E. 2013. "Russia's Elite: What They Think of the United States and Why." *PONARS Eurasia Policy Memo* No. 273, August.

Popkova, A. 2017. "'Putin Is Playing Chess and I Think We Are Playing Marbles.' Vladimir Putin's 'Soft Power' and the American Right." *International Communication Gazette* 79 (April). http://journals.sagepub.com/doi/abs/10.1177/1748048516688133.

Porter, G. 2017. "How 'New Cold Warriors' Cornered Trump." *Consortiumnews.com*, February 25.

Pratt, S. F. 2017. "A Relational View of Ontological Security in International Relations." *International Studies Quarterly* 61, no. 1: 78–85.

Rabotyazhev, N. 2013. "Rossiyskaya natsional'naya identichnost' v zerkale sovremennogo otechesetvennogo konservaizma." *Politiya* 70, no. 3: 62–84.

Raimondo, J. 2017. "Rush to Judgment: The Evidence That the Russians Hacked the DNC Is Collapsing." *Antiwar.com*, March 24.

Raimondo, J. 2018. "The New Cold War Is Here." *Antiwar.com*, March 5.

Reus-Smit, C. 1999. *The Moral Purpose of the State: Culture, Social Identity, and Institutional Rationality in International Relations*. Princeton, NJ: Princeton University Press.

Reynolds, V., V. Falgar, and I. Vine, eds. 1987. *The Sociobiology of Ethnocentrism: Evolutionary Dimensions of Xenophobia, Discrimination, Racism and Nationalism*. London: Croom Helm.

Robertson, G. 2011. *The Politics of Protest in Hybrid Regimes: Managing Dissent in Post-Communist Russia*. Cambridge: Cambridge University Press.

Robinson, P. 2002. *The CNN Effect: The Myth of News, Foreign Policy and Intervention*. London: Routledge.

Royce, E. 2015. "Countering Putin's Information Weapons of War." *Wall Street Journal*, April 15.

Russia's Wrong Direction: What the United States Can and Should Do. 2006. New York: Council on Foreign Relations.

Rutland, P. 2017. "Trump, Putin, and the Future of US-Russian Relations." *Slavic Review*, August.

Ryan, M. 2004. "Framing the War against Terrorism: US Newspaper Editorials and Military Action in Afghanistan." *International Communication Gazette* 66, no. 5: 363–82.

Saff, S. and Y. Ohara. 2006. "The Media and the Pursuit of Militarism in Japan." *Critical Discourse Studies* 3, no. 1: 81–101.

Safire, W. 1994. "Strategic Dilemma." *New York Times*, December 1.

Said, E. W. 1978. *Orientalism*. New York: Vintage Books.

Said, E. W. 1997. *Covering Islam: How the Media and the Experts Determine How We See the Rest of the World*. Rev. ed. New York: Vintage Books.

Sakwa, R. 2012. "Conspiracy Narratives as a Mode of Engagement in International Politics: The Case of the 2008 Russo-Georgian War." *Russian Review* 71, no. 4: 551–64.

Saul, N. 1991. *Distant Friends: The United States and Russia, 1763–1867*. Lawrence: University Press of Kansas.

Schrad, M. L. 2017. "Vladimir Putin Isn't a Supervillain." *Foreign Policy*, March 2.
Sergunin, A. and L. Karabeshkin. 2015. "Understanding Russia's Soft Power Strategy." *Politics* 35, nos. 3–4: 347–63.
Sharafutdinova, G. 2014. "The Pussy Riot Affair and Putin's Démarche from Sovereign Democracy to Sovereign Morality." *Nationalities Papers* 42, no. 4: 615–21.
Shlapentokh, V. 2011. "The Puzzle of Russian Anti-Americanism: From 'Below' or from 'Above.'" *Europe-Asia Studies* 63, no. 5: 875–89.
Simons, G. 2010. *Mass Media and Modern Warfare: Reporting on the Russian War on Terrorism*. London: Routledge.
Simons, G. 2015. "Aspects of Putin's Appeal to International Public." *Global Affairs* 1, no. 2: 205–08.
Simons, G. 2018. "Media and Public Diplomacy." In A. Tsygankov, ed., *The Routledge Handbook of Russian Foreign Policy*. London: Routledge.
Smith, K. C. and M. Wakefield. 2005. "Textual Analysis of Tobacco Editorials." *American Journal of Health Promotion* 19, no. 5: 361–68.
Smith, N. R. 2018. "The Re-emergence of a 'Mirror Image' in West-Russia Relations?" *International Politics* 55: 575–94.
Snyder, T. 2014. "Putin's New Nostalgia." *New York Review of Books*, November 10.
Snyder, T. 2017. "We Lost a War: Russia's Interference in Our Election Was Much More Than Simple Mischief-Making." *New York Daily News*, March 19.
Soldatov, A. 2016. "Reading the World: The Internet and Political Change in Russia." *Foreign Affairs*, April 6. https://www.foreignaffairs.com/articles/russian-federation/2016-04-06/reading-world.
Sorgin, V. 1996. "Zapadny liberalizm i rossiyskiye reformy." *Svobodnaya mysl'* 1: 32–44.
Steele, B. J. 2008. *Ontological Security in International Relations*. London: Routledge.
Stent, A. 2014. *Limits of Partnership: US-Russian Relations in the Twenty-First Century*. Princeton, NJ: Princeton University Press.
Surkov, V. 2006. "Suvrenitet—eto politicheskiy sinonim konkurentosposobnosti." *Moscow News*, March 3.
Tolz, V. and S. Hutchins. 2015. *Nation, Ethnicity, and Race on Russian Television: Mediating Post-Soviet Differences*. London: Routledge.
Toynbee, A. 1948. *Civilization on Trial*. Oxford: Oxford University Press.
Trenin, D. 2006. *Intregatsiya i identichnost'*. Moscow: Tsentr Karnegi.
Trenin, D. 2015. *Rossiya i mir v XXI veke*. Moscow: Aspekt Press.
Tsvetkova, N. A. 2015. "Publichnaya diplomatiya SShA." *Mezhdunarodnyye protsessy* 13, no. 3: 121–33.
Tsygankov, A. P. 2004. *Whose World Order? Russia's Perception of American Ideas after the Cold War*. South Bend, IN: University of Notre Dame Press.
Tsygankov, A. P. 2009. *Anti-Russian Lobby and American Foreign Policy*. London: Palgrave.

Tsygankov, A. P. 2012. *Russia and the West from Alexander to Putin.* Cambridge: Cambridge University Press.

Tsygankov, A. P. 2012. "Assessing Cultural and Regime-Based Explanations of Russia's Foreign Policy." *Europe-Asia Studies* 64: 695–713.

Tsygankov, A. P. 2015. "Russia's Soft Power Strategy." *Current History* 112.

Tsygankov, A. P. 2015. *The Strong State in Russia: Development and Crisis.* Oxford: Oxford University Press.

Tsygankov, A. P. 2016. "Crafting the State-Civilization: Vladimir Putin's Turn to Distinct Values." *Problems of Post-Communism* 63, no. 3: 146–58.

Tsygankov, A. P. 2016. "The Dark Double: The American Media Perception of Russia as a Neo-Soviet Autocracy, 2008–2014." *Politics* 37, no. 1: 19–35.

Tsygankov, A. P. 2016. *Russia's Foreign Policy: Change and Continuity in National Identity*, 4th ed. Boulder, CO: Rowman & Littlefield.

Tsygankov, A. P. 2017. "Russia's Limited Information War on the West." *Public Diplomacy*, June 5.

Tsygankov, A. P. and D. Parker. 2015. "The Securitization of Democracy: Freedom House Ratings of Russia." *European Security.*

Tuminez, A. S. 2000. *Russian Nationalism since 1856: Ideology and the Making of Foreign Policy.* Boulder, CO: Rowman & Littlefield.

Turner, O. 2013. "'Threatening' China and US Security: The International Politics of Identity." *Review of International Studies* 39: 903–24.

Valeriano, B., B. Jensen, and R. C. Maness. 2018. *Cyber Strategy: The Evolving Character of Power and Coercion.* New York: Oxford University Press.

Van Herpen, M. H. 2015. *Putin's Propaganda Machine.* Boulder, CO: Rowman & Littlefield.

Van Herpen, M. H. 2015. *Putin's Wars: The Rise of Russia's New Imperialism.* Boulder, CO: Rowman & Littlefield.

Virgil. 2016. "The Real Siberian Candidate and the Deep State." *Breitbart*, December 19.

Volkov, D. 2015. "The Evolution of Anti-Americanism in Russia." *Carnegie.ru* Commentary, June 22. http://carnegieendowment.org/2015/06/22/evolution-of-anti-americanism-in-russia/iavh.

Von Seth, R. 2018. "All Quiet on the Eastern Front? Media Images of the West and Russian Foreign Political Identity." *Europe-Asia Studies* 70: 421–40.

Wald, K. D. and A. Calhoun-Brown. 2014. *Religion and Politics in the United States.* Boulder, CO: Rowman & Littlefield.

Walker, J. 2017. "Is the Trump-Russia Story an Octopus or Spaghetti?" *Los Angeles Times*, March 24.

Walt, S. M. 2016. "The Collapse of the Liberal World Order." *Foreign Policy*, June 26.

Warren, C. 2014. "Not by the Sword Alone: Soft Power, Mass Media, and the Production of State Sovereignty." *International Organization* 68, no. 1: 111–41.

White, D. 2018. "State Capacity and Regime Resilience in Putin's Russia." *International Political Science Review* 39, no. 1: 130–43. http://journals.sagepub.com/doi/abs/10.1177/0192512117694481.

Wilson, A. 2005. *Virtual Democracy: Faking Democracy in the Post-Soviet World*. New Haven: Yale University Press.

Wilson, J. L. 2015. "Russia and China Respond to Soft Power: Interpretation and Readaptation of a Western Construct." *Politics* 35, nos. 3–4: 287–300.

Yablokov, I. 2015. "Conspiracy Theories as a Russian Public Diplomacy Tool: The Case of Russia Today. RT." *Politics* 35: 301–15.

Zaharna, R. S. 2010. *Battles to Bridges: US Strategic Communication and Public Diplomacy after 9/11*. Basingstoke: Palgrave Macmillan.

Zakaria, F. 1997. "Illiberal Democracy." *Foreign Affairs*, November–December.

Zarakol, A. 2010. *After Defeat: How the East Learned to Live with the West*. Cambridge: Cambridge University Press.

Ziegler, C. 2014. "Russian-American Relations: From Tsarism to Putin." *International Politics* 51, no. 6: 671–92.

Ziegler, C. 2017. "International Dimensions of Electoral Processes: Russia, the USA, and the 2016 Elections." *International Politics* 54 (October): 1–17.

Zielonka, J. 2012. "Empire and Modern Geopolitical System." *Geopolitics* 17: 502–25.

Zimmerman, W. 2002. *The Russian People and Foreign Policy*. Princeton, NJ: Princeton University Press.

Zimmerman, W. 2014. *Ruling Russia: Authoritarianism from the Revolution to Putin*. Princeton, NJ: Princeton University Press.

INDEX

adoption of Russian children, 71
Air Force One (film), 36
American fears of Russia. *See* Russophobia
American values. *See* "universal"
   Western values
anti-Russian lobbies, 24, 33, 46, 49–50, 102
Antonov, Mikhail, 134n56
Applebaum, Anne, 54–55, 83–84
al-Assad, Bashar, 85–86, 91
Assange, Julian, 69, 102–3

Baker, Peter: *Kremlin Rising*, 47
Baltic nations on Soviet victory in
   WWII, 129n60
BBG (Broadcasting Board of Governors),
   30–31, 55–56
Bennett, W. Lance, 20–21
Berezovski, Boris, 74–75
"black dossier" on Trump, 84–85
Bolshevik revolution (1917), 2, 24
Bolton, John, 87–88
Bolton, Richard, 85–86
Bout, Victor, 69
Breitbart on Trump-Russia collusion
   narrative, 86–87
Britain
   diplomats expelled from Russia, 131n79
   Russian diplomats expelled from, 79–80
Broadcasting Board of Governors (BBG),
   30–31, 55–56
Brzezinski, Zbigniew, 36–37, 120n8
Buchanan, Patrick, 7
Burr, Richard, 84–85
Bush, George H. W., 20–21
Bush, George W.
   anti-Russian narratives exploited by, 102
   liberal democratic values and, 81
   on Putin, 108
   regime change strategy of, 5, 102
   US-Russia cooperation under, 46, 49

Cardin, Ben, 92
Carnegie Moscow Center, 54–55
Carr, E. H., 103–4
Castells, Manuel, 18–19
censorship, 73
Center for American Progress, 91–92
centralization of power
   checks and balances vs., 2, 3
   "universal" Western values vs., 26–27
   US media on, 26, 38
   US State Department on, 30
"chaos" narrative (1995–2005), 36–37
Chechnya
   Russian war in, 36–37, 58, 93
   Yeltsin's foreign policy and, 78–79
checks and balances, 2, 3, 11–12, 70–71
Cheney, Dick, 46–47, 92
China, US dominance challenged by, 107–8
Christianity, 4, 11–12, 103–4
Clapper, James, 52
Clinton, Bill
   on Chechen war, 36–37
   liberal democratic values and, 81
   Yeltsin supported by, 36
Clinton, Hillary
   email controversy and, 90–91
   on Eurasian union attempt, 51–52
   Hard Choices, 91
   propaganda and media strategy, 30–31,
      50–51, 93, 94
   Russian ties of, 93–94
   Trump's Russia perspective and, 83, 90–91
   US media on, 104
   WikiLeaks and, 27
Cohen, Stephen F., 7, 35, 48–49, 114n29, 123n51
Cold War. *See also* new cold war
   as historical trauma, 93, 99–100
   Russian independence narrative and, 73–74
   US government influence on media
      during, 28

153

Cold War (*cont.*)
  US media response following, 20–21, 29
  values conflict in, 24–25, 33–34
  Western perceptions of Russia and, 2, 42
collusion. *See* Trump-Russia collusion narrative
Conaway, Mike, 84–85
cooperation and joint solutions
  in cyber area, 96
  ethno-phobic lobbies and, 20
  following September 11 terrorist attacks, 25–26, 74
  national trauma and, 17–18, 24–25, 73–74
  in new international system, 105
  soft power and, 106
  Trump on, 82–83
  US media resistance to, 3–5, 14
  in values relations, 100–1
corruption
  Putin's Secret Riches and, 113n20
  Russian struggles with, 4, 36, 59–60
  US perception of Russia and, 14, 25–26, 30, 36
Council on Foreign Relations, 46–47
Crimea, annexation of, 6, 27, 30, 52, 53–54, 75–77, 79, 82–83, 90
critics of Russian government, criminal trials of, 14
cultural reformulation, 106
cyber and espionage activities, 52, 84, 85–86, 90–91, 103

deep state, 86–87, 98–99
Democratic National Committee, cyberattacks against, 27, 84, 90, 93–94
democratic values. *See* "universal" Western values
diktat, 97–98
Duma, 30, 59–60

editorials, convergence of attitudes in, 39, 120n17, 40n*
editors, influence of, 20, 33
Ekho Moskvy (radio station), 41–42
elections
  falsification of, in Russia, 14, 41, 59–60
  Russian 2018 presidential election, 79
  Russian interference in Ukrainian elections, 46–47
  Russian media on, 70–71
  US presidential election (2016). *See* Trump-Russia collusion narrative
Engel, Elliot, 31

Ernest, John, 113n20
ethnocentrism, 9–10, 17, 23
  Cold War propaganda and, 28
  media focus on, 9–10
  in neo-Soviet autocracy narrative, 38
  in Putin's values framing, 75–76
  social identity theory and, 116n2
  in US media, 62
Eurasian union, attempts to create, 51–52, 69–70
Euromaidan revolution (2014), 6, 22, 27, 51–52

Facebook, Russian activity on, 55–56, 84–85
family values, 71, 75–76
fear and suspicion. *See also* Russophobia
  government manipulation of, 21–22, 93
  in media, 17–18, 20
  in "neo-Soviet autocracy" narrative, 26–27
  propaganda reflecting, 22
financial crisis (2008), 89–90
Flynn, Michael, 31–32, 134n56
Foglesong, David, 2
"foreign enemy" narrative (2014–2016), 52–55, 82
Fox News on Trump-Russia collusion narrative, 86–87
frames and framing devices, 10, 39, 41. *See also* Russian media; US media
France, Iraq War and, 107–8, 136–37n18
Freedom House, 28, 46–47, 62
Friedman, Thomas, 49–50, 83–84
Frye, Timothy, 79
Fukuyama, Francis, 33–34, 64–65

Gaidar, Yegor, 66–67
gays and lesbians, 14, 42–43, 49–50, 71–72, 120–21n18
Georgia
  NATO expansion and, 87–88
  Russian intervention in, 30, 38, 66–67, 93
  US diplomatic relations with, 48, 66–67, 69
Germany, Iraq War and, 107–8
Gessen, Masha, 89, 114n30
Glasser, Susan: *Kremlin Rising*, 47
global financial crisis (2008), 89–90
globalization
  criticism of, 87
  in media, 9
  national identities under, 101
  Russian political system and, 61
  "universal" Western values in, 38
Gorbachev, Mikhail, 64–65
Graham, Lindsey, 83–84
Greenwald, Glenn, 7, 87–88, 114n29

Group of Eight, 44–46, 48
Gusinski, Vladimir, 74–75

Hafez, Kari, 9
Haley, Nikki, 87–88
Heritage Foundation, 54–55
Hofstadter, Richard, 93
homosexuality. *See* gays and lesbians
Hounshell, Blake, 89
human rights issues
  absent state conflict, 108
  asset freezes and, 51–52
  Cold War and, 28
  in future global conflict, 107
  Gorbachev and, 64–65
  managed democracy and, 51–52
  Obama's prioritization of, 5
  Russian foreign policy and, 60
  US foreign policy and, 107–8
Human Rights Watch, 28
Hussein, Saddam, 66–67

indexing news coverage, 20–21
individualism
  as American value, 2–3, 24–25
  from Protestant tradition, 11–12
  in Russian media, 65, 100
  Russian political system and, 61, 78
information wars
  American fear of Russia and, 22, 27, 54–55, 104
  Clinton on, 30–31, 50–51
  "foreign enemy" narrative and, 52
  International Communication Reform Act (2014) and, 52
  Russian effectiveness in, 55–56
  Russian motivation for, 96
  Russia Today vs. Radio Free Europe/Radio Liberty, 55
  US counters to, 29–30
  Western values in, 50–51
Institute of Modern Russia, 55
interference in elections. *See* elections; Trump-Russia collusion narrative
International Communications Reform Act (2014), 31, 52
international competition
  culture wars and, 106
  effects of, 10, 18
  future clashes in, 105
  ideological conflict in, 12, 14–15, 105–6, 107
  media's role in, 100
  national traumas and, 18

propaganda and, 22, 28
values' role in, 8, 12, 107
Iran, US dominance challenged by, 107–8
Iraq War, 21, 66–67, 89–90, 107–8
Islamism vs. secularism, 105–6
Islamophobia, 70–71

Jefferson, Thomas, 23
Jews, anti-Russian lobbying by, 24
Jilani, Zaid, 87–88
journalists. *See also* media systems
  Chechen war and, 36–37
  elite political figures and, 20–21
  neo-Soviet autocracy narrative and, 47
  on Russia adopting Western values, 36
  US funding for, in Russia, 30, 50–51

Keller, Bill, 49–50
Kennan, George, 24, 95, 118n24
Kennedy, Daniel, 55–56
Kerry, John, 31
Khodorkovsky, Mikhail, 41–42, 55
Kislyak, Sergei, 31–32, 92–93, 134n56
Kozyrev, Andrei, 2–3
Kristof, Nicholas, 83–84
Krugman, Paul, 83, 94

Leupp, Gary, 87–88
Libya, regime change in, 69
Lieven, Anatol, 99–100
limited democracy, 61–62
Litvinenko, Alexander, 43, 121–22n29
Lucas, Edward, 54–55

Maddow, Rachel, 83–84, 85–86
Magnitsky Law, 48, 50, 51–52
Maidan Revolution. *See* Euromaidan Revolution
managed democracy, 61–62
Manheim, Karl, 1
Manifest Destiny, 24
market democracy, 4–5, 34, 65, 78–79, 103–4
Markov, Sergei, 71–72
Matlock, Jack, 7
McCain, John, 46–47, 83–84, 92
McFaul, Michael
  on aggressiveness of US policy towards Russia, 27, 48, 54–55
  on isolating Russia, 6
  on Russian domestic policies, 5–6
  on Russian threat, 83
  on Trump-Russia collusion narrative, 83–84

INDEX | 155

Mead, Walter Russell, 86–87
media systems. *See also* Russian media;
US media
    autonomy of, 10–11, 28, 97–98
    ethnocentrism in, 9–10
    exploitation of, 20
    government manipulation of, 20–22
    narrative framing in, 10, 18–19
    propaganda in, 52
    role of, 9, 99–100
    threat responses of, 18–20
    values and, 1–2, 9, 18–19
    in Western-style political systems, 63–64
Medvedev, Dmitry
    nuclear arms control and, 5, 44
    protests against, 59–60
    Putin compared to, 122n44
    on state control of historical narrative, 75
    US media on, 39, 48
    US perception of Russia and, 69
    US-Russia rapprochement and, 47–48, 49, 56, 102–3, 108
Mueller, Robert, 84–85, 89
Murdoch, Rupert, 21
Myers, Steven Lee: *Russian Roulette*, 89

narratives in media, 9–10. *See also* Russian media; US media; *specific narratives*
national identities and beliefs
    American crisis of, 89–90, 104
    destabilizing potential of, 105
    under globalization, 101
    historical trauma and, 17–18
    international relations and, 1–2
    media's influence on, 99–100
    software and, 106
    values in, 17, 18–19
nationalism
    ethnic, 106
    exploitation of, 20, 104, 105
    sources of, 10, 11, 28
NATO
    isolation of Russia and, 48, 73–74, 87–88
    Russian expansionism and, 36–37
    Yugoslavia crisis and, 19–20, 36, 66–67
Navalny, Alexei, 41–42
Nazis, as Russian media villains, 54–55, 75, 76–77
neo-Soviet autocracy narrative (2005–2013), 3–4, 13–14
    American identity and, 99–100
    excessive/reductionist nature of, 4, 41–44, 57–58, 60–61, 62–63, 64

    government exploitation of, 102
    interstate tensions and, 44–52, 56
    media frames for, 38–44
    US media default to, 56
new cold war
    Crimea annexation and, 6
    values confrontation in, 2, 46, 105–6
New York Times and perceptions of Russia, 39–44, 67–69, 120–21n18, 128n31
Nezavisimaya gazeta (NG) and perceptions of United States, 67–70, 128n31
nuclear capabilities in US-Russia relations, 4–5
Nuland, Victoria, 50–51
Nye, Joseph, 106

Obama, Barack
    conservative US media on, 87
    DNC hacking and, 91–92
    liberal democratic values and, 81
    on Russian domestic policies, 5
    on Russian foreign policy, 91
    Russian policy shift by, 29–31
    Snowden's asylum and, 51–52
    State of the Union address (2014), 51–52
    US-Russia rapprochement and, 47–48, 49, 102, 108
oil and oil prices, 58–59
oligarchs and oligarchy, 58, 63–64, 70–71, 78–79
Olympics (Sochi 2014), 49–50
"others"
    fear and, 18, 22
    maintaining national confidence, 99–101
    in national and media narratives, 9–10, 13, 22, 26, 28, 81
    US media dependence on, 118n28
    values defined against, 2, 81
Owen, Robert, 121–22n29

Panarin, Igor', 135–36n4
Parry, Robert, 7
perestroika, 64–65
Petraeus, David H., 52
Pipes, Richard, 37
Polity IV, 62
Pomerantsev, Peter, 54–55
Pompeo, Michael, 87–88
Presidential Council for Civil Society and Human Rights (Russia), 61–62
Primakov, Yevgeny, 78–79
propaganda
    characterization of, 22

International Communications Reform Act (2014) and, 52
media autonomy and, 10–11
Obama's Russia policy and, 30–31, 50, 52
in Russian media, 12–13, 29–30
of Russian state, 54–55, 57, 58, 77–78
in US foreign policy, 69
US media dismissing dissenting voices as, 88–89
Protestantism, 11–12
public support in foreign relations, 8–9, 65
Pussy Riot, 41–42, 71
Putin, Vladimir
anti-terrorism aid to United States, 19, 74
Bush on, 108
Clinton on, 91
conservative US media on, 87
on democracy and the strong state, 78–79
domestic politics and, 8, 38, 47–48
on executive authority, 3
Federation Council speech (2005), 74–75
Federation Council speech (2013), 75–76
foreign policy, 38
Litvinenko assassination and, 121–22n29
Medvedev compared to, 122n44
in neo-Soviet autocracy narrative, 38, 42–43
pardons issued by, 41–42
re-election of (March 2018), 79
Royce on, 55
Russophobia and, 31
support for, 43–44, 53–54, 58, 74, 77–78, 79, 124–25n75
Trump on, 82–83
Trump-Russia collusion narrative and, 7, 82, 83–87, 88–89, 93–94
US challenges to, 5–6, 48
US media's portrayal of, 3–4, 26, 27, 49–50, 53, 57–58, 98
on US military intervention in Iraq, 38
on US political system, 135n1
on US presidential election campaign (2016), 27
values framing by, 75–76, 129–30n63
Putin's Secret Riches (documentary), 113n20

Radio Free Europe/Radio Liberty, 30–31, 55
Raimondo, Justin, 87–88
religious freedom, 2, 11–12
Ren TV, 41–42
Roosevelt, Theodore, 24
Rossotrudichestvo (Russian Cooperation), 76
Royce, Ed, 31, 55

RT. *See* Russia Today
Rumsfeld, Donald, 107–8
Russia
anti-Americanism in, 8, 14, 44–46, 58, 65–66, 97–99
British diplomats expelled from, 131n79
centralization of power in, 2, 3, 26–27, 36, 41, 56, 77–78
conspiracy theories on Western intent, 126n9
cybersecurity and, 96
defense as motivation for, 95–96, 103
economic development and, 58, 79, 126n4
expansionism and, 6
fear of United States, 136n9
financial collapse, 36
foreign policy, 44, 56, 57, 60, 64, 76
fraudulent elections in, 14, 41
great-power status and, 43–44, 73–74, 75, 87, 96, 100, 101–2
historical challenges to, 62
media autonomy in, 41–42, 61–62, 78–79. *See also* Russian media
minorities in, 26, 41, 58, 61–62, 71–72
political and administrative system in, 43, 57–59, 60–63, 74–75, 78
political opposition within, 30, 38, 41, 47–48, 59–60, 61–62, 74–75, 78–79
sanctions against. *See* sanctions
social welfare and development, 58
state-media relations in, 72–73, 76
support for the state in, 43–44
as threat to the West, 57–58
transition to market democracy, 33–35
values framing in, 74–78, 129–30n63
Western values in, 2–3, 29, 57–58, 64–67
Russiagate. *See* Trump-Russia collusion narrative
Russian constitution (1993), 3, 78–79
Russian Cooperation (Rossotrudichestvo), 76
Russian Idea, 13
Russian media
anti-Americanism in, 19–20, 67, 72–73, 97–98, 99–100
on anti-terrorism aid to US, 19, 67, 74
indigenous Russian values and, 67
Nazis in, 54–55, 75, 76–77
opponents discredited in, 8–9
Russian identity and, 100
on traditional family values, 71
on Trump, 98–99
on Ukrainian revolution (2014), 22
on US domestic policy, 70–72

Russian media (*cont.*)
  on US foreign policy, 67–70
  on US global dominance, 98–99
  on Western support for Georgia, 66–67
  on Western values, 65, 70–72
  Yugoslavia crisis (1999) and, 19–20
Russian Orthodox Church, 76
Russia Today (RT), 30–31, 54–55, 76
Russo-Japanese War, 24
Russophobia
  American dream vs. Russian Idea, 13
  American identity and, 104
  cyber vulnerability, 86
  development of, 23–27, 30–31
  election interference, 27
  in Europe, 24
  expansionism, 27, 30, 53
  "foreign enemy" narrative and, 52, 54–55
  intensity of, 89
  Leupp on, 87–88
  neo-Soviet autocracy narrative from, 38, 42
  policy influence of, 24
  Russian media on, 70
  "transition" narrative failure and, 37
  Trump-Russia collusion narrative and, 14, 89–93
Rwandan genocide (1992), 107

Saakashvili, Mikheil, 66–67, 69
Safire, William, 36–37
Said, Edward, 9–10
sanctions
  Clinton on, 91
  Crimea annexation and, 6, 51–52, 53
  Putin's popular support and, 79–80
  Russian media on, 70
  Trump on, 6, 82–83
  US media advocating for, 98
Schrad, Mark, 95
secularism vs. radical Islamism, 105–6
September 11, 2001 terrorist attacks. *See* terrorism and September 11, 2001 terrorist attacks
Sestanovich, Steven, 27
Skrypal, Sergei, 79–80
Snowden, Edward, 50, 69, 103
Snyder, Timothy, 83
Sochi Olympics (2014), 49–50
social identity theory, 116n2
social networks, 55–56, 84–85, 86
"soft power" as political competition, 8, 21–22, 76, 106–7

sovereign democracy, 74–75
Specter, Michael, 34–35
Steele, Christopher, 84–85
strategy of influence, 21–22, 29
strong state. *See also* centralization of power
  administration of, 59
  effectiveness of, 63
  Orange Revolution (2004) and, 44–46
  Putin on, 3
  as response to Western pressure, 103–4
  Russian pride in, 43–44, 53–54
  traditional values of, 77–78
Surkov, Vladislav, 74–75
Syria
  Clinton on, 91
  US and Turkey on, 108
  US missile strikes against, 85–86

Talbott, Strobe, 53–54
terrorism and September 11, 2001 terrorist attacks, 5, 6, 19, 25–26, 67, 74, 82–83, 89–90, 108
Tillerson, Rex, 85–86
Toynbee, Arnold, 114n31
traditional family values, 71, 75–76
trauma, national and historical, 17–18
Trump, Donald
  America-first principle of, 113n23
  on "Arab NATO," 108
  "black dossier" on, 84–85
  on Clinton's emails, 90–91
  expulsion of diplomats by, 85–86
  on global institutions, 84
  liberal establishment on, 6, 31–32, 81
  missile strikes against Syria, 85–86
  perspective on Russia, 82–83, 85–86, 87, 90, 93
  on Putin, 82–83, 131n3
  values relations and, 6–7
Trump-Russia collusion narrative, 81–86
  American values and, 89–90
  as Democrats' effort to derail Trump, 94–95
  Gessen on, 114n30
  liberal self maintained through, 99–100
  opposition to, 86–89
  political divide at root of, 104
  Russia's role in, 93–96
  Russophobia and, 27, 89–93, 95
  as US media bias, 83, 98
tsarist system, 42, 57–58, 62–63, 73, 77–78, 103–4
Turkey, 108
Twitter, Russian activity on, 55–56, 84–85

Ukraine
  Euromaidan revolution (2014), 6, 22, 27, 51–52
  Nuland on, 50–51
  Orange Revolution (2004), 38, 44–46
  Russian media on, 70
  Russian public opinion on intervention in, 124–25n75
  Russian support for separatists in, 52–53, 90
  US media on, 48, 53
  US-Russia tension and, 53–55, 87–88, 91, 93
United Nations (UN)
  cyber area and, 96
  Yugoslavia crisis and, 19–20
United States (US). *See also* Russophobia; *specific presidents*
  anti-Russian attitudes in, 8, 102–3
  checks and balances in, 2, 11–12, 70–71
  covert activities in foreign policy, 95
  cyber tools for assertive foreign policy and, 103
  ethnocentrism in, 23–24
  fear of Russia, 13, 102
  funding for media outlets in Russia, 30
  Georgia supported by, 66–67, 69
  global reputation of, 29, 89–90
  imposition of values by, 23–26, 95
  Iraq War and, 21, 66–67, 89–90, 107–8
  media autonomy in, 10–11, 28
  media influence of, 20–21, 28–32, 50
  Middle East policy, 108
  missile defense system in Europe, 44
  regime change strategy of, 5, 102, 106
  Russia policy shifts, 4–6, 13–14, 49
  values divide within, 6, 14, 33, 81, 89–90, 91–92, 94–95
"universal" Western values
  "chaos" narrative and, 37
  Cold War and, 2–3, 28
  executive authority vs., 26–27
  ideological divisions from, 46–47, 60–61
  international competition and, 12–13, 30–31, 50–51
  "neo-Soviet autocracy" narrative and, 44–46, 49–50
  Russian attitudes toward, 64–67
  Russian media on, 70–72
  Soviet oppression vs., 24–25
  "transition" narrative and, 33–35
  Trump's election calling into question, 81
  World War II and, 11–12

US media. *See also* neo-Soviet autocracy narrative; Trump-Russia collusion narrative
  American superiority in, 4, 9–10, 13
  anti-Russian bias in, 11–12, 97–98, 99–100
  on anti-terrorism cooperation, 25–26
  "chaos" narrative (1995–2005), 36–37
  Cold War propaganda in, 24–25, 28
  convergence of attitudes in, 39
  failings of, 57–58, 61, 62, 88–89
  "foreign enemy" narrative (2014–2016), 52–55, 82, 97–98
  government influence on, 20–21, 28–32, 50
  Iraq War and, 21, 107–8
  liberal views dominant in, 26–27
  on Litvinenko poisoning, 43
  narratives of otherness and, 118n28
  "paranoid style" in, 93
  political influence of, 8–9, 13–14, 48, 49–50, 51–52
  propaganda model and, 10–11
  public perception of Russia and, 56
  on Putin, 77–78, 97–98
  on Russia as threat to values, 3–4, 5, 82, 95
  Russian history in, 42, 57–58
  Soviets as ideological "other" in, 2
  "transition to democracy" narrative (early 1990s), 25–26, 29–30, 33–35, 56
  Trump-Russia collusion narrative and, 81–89
  Trump's Russia perspective exploited by, 83, 98
  voices of dissent in, 7, 13–14, 48–49, 86–89, 104

values relations, 1, 17. *See also* "universal" Western values
  centrality of, 5, 7
  Cold War and, 24–25
  future clashes in, 105–8
  history of, 2–4, 11–12, 24–27, 97–98
  international competition and, 8
  interstate tensions from, 14, 37, 44–52, 72–73, 97
  as irreconcilable opposition, 37, 101–2
  political explanations for/manipulations of, 7–8, 20–21, 73, 94–95, 100–4
  reframing, 7
  Russian media and, 72–73, 99–100
  Trump and, 6–7, 14, 31–32
  US media biases and, 11–12, 99–100
  US policy and, 4–6, 13–14
Villepin, Dominique de, 136–37n18

Walker, Jesse, 93–94
Wall Street Journal and neo-Soviet autocracy narrative, 39–44, 120–21n18
Washington Post and neo-Soviet autocracy narrative, 38–44, 120–21n18
WikiLeaks, 27, 50, 88–89

Yanukovich, Victor, 76–77
Yavlinsky, Grigory, 34–35
Yeltsin, Boris, 34–36, 78–79, 131n74
Yugoslavia crisis (1999), 19–20, 36, 66–67

一

Printed and bound by CPI Group (UK) Ltd, Croydon, CR0 4YY